The 8 Stories for Businesses & Professionals

A new way of looking at individual and organizational narrative needs in the 21st century from India's leading storytelling organization

Michael Burns, Ph.D.

The 8 Stories for Businesses & Professionals

ISBN: 978-1-7355349-6-1

First impression 2020

10 9 8 7 6 5 4 3 2 1

1

The 8 Stories for Businesses & Professionals

A new way of looking at individual and organizational narrative needs in the 21st century from India's leading storytelling organization

Michael Burns is an author university professor, award-winning documentary filmmaker, and writing coach. He's the founder of Tall Tales, India's longest-running live nonfiction storytelling series, which conducts performances, workshops, retreats, and corporate trainings on story design and brand enhancement. He's the author of *Hack into your Creativity* (Penguin, 2017) and the editor of *The Best of Tall Tales* (Rupa, 2018). He splits his time between the US and India. More on his work can be found at writewithmichael.com.

Contents:

Introduction

    The Base

    The Maker

    The Vision

    The Product

    The Springboard

    The Morale Builder

    The Capsule

    The Talk

Introduction

We've all heard that storytelling is the most important tool in the business communicator's toolbox. But there are some other things that we haven't heard enough about—and this book fills those gaps. Specifically, we haven't heard enough about two things: 1) what a story is in the first place; and 2) the fact that you can't just take a story and make it the centerpiece of a business presentation and expect a panacea: context is crucial and details matter.

To take on the first of those, you might be saying to yourself, *I know what a story is. Do we really need to spend time going over that?* The answer is yes. I remember many years ago reading one of the most important books on business storytelling and coming across a curious passage near the beginning declaring that the author would not open the ideological "can of worms" about what a story is, since there's no consensus about its definition. I found this jaw-dropping and began to question the integrity of the entire rest of the text. Far from trivial, this question is not only crucial, it's *unavoidable* for anyone looking at this subject with any level of seriousness. This book takes this question head on, gently at first and then specifically after that.

And to take on the second idea (that story context matters), the heart of this book's thesis is that stories are not a one-size-fits-all addition to any presentation. It's not like speech surgery where you open a presentation and insert a story and expect that everything will be fine. Stories *are* critical and they *are* powerful.

But as the situations where they're needed change, the stories themselves must change in turn. This book is about how to make those context-driven modifications and still get the most impact out of your storytelling.

As I touch on in the pages to come, storytelling is our species' superpower and it's both instructive and inspiring to see the amount of storytelling analysis happening all around us. In researching for this book, I digested observations from over 25 leading texts on business storytelling and communication. I made a wide survey of the key contributions to academic literature over the last ten years on the subject. And I watched over 200 live or video presentations that integrate storytelling in order to study the details of what presenters do and how they do it. The patterns I noticed and the dots I connected are shared throughout the pages that follow.

The ideas that I'm sharing in this book stem from my own personal experience in several dimensions of storytelling. I was the first student in the history of the United Kingdom to successfully submit an audio/visual doctorate where I looked at the forms and limits of story design in documentary film. During my studies and in the years that followed, I made five films for international television before finding my most heartfelt passion: story structure. I began writing but simultaneously looking closely at the mechanics of writing and story construction in particular. My informal work suddenly coalesced when I founded Tall Tales in 2015, three years after moving to India from my native US.

4

Tall Tales began as one night of Moth-style live, personal, nonfiction storytelling, but unexpectedly grew into something much more. The initial idea was to collect funny, dramatic, and/or tragic first-hand experiences and have the storytellers share those alone at a microphone in front of an audience. But instead of just one night, the positive response prompted us to do two... then three... then five... and then ten. As of this writing, our next show will be our 78th show and there are no signs of slowing down as the story submissions continue to come in. Parallel to these live performances, I also designed then delivered a workshop on story structure and writing best-practice in general. Again, a temporary side-project turned into something else, and I've now delivered hundreds of workshops on storytelling on four continents that also include corporate, educational, public and private classes, trainings, retreats, and online modules.

I think it's important that I'm interested in a wide range of storytelling modalities. I'm not focused on one slice of the field, but have and continue to put my thumb in sub-fields that offer their own unique flavor of experience. Film and visual storytelling stimulate my mind while written storytelling nurtures my soul and sustains me. From fiction to nonfiction and from micro stories to epic sagas, I have an interest in all of them even if I appreciate some slightly more than others. There are sensibilities to be gained from each of these traditions, aspects that we can bring to bear on the stories we are creating right now for work and for fun. The maps made by those who've traveled before us have so much to teach, and the more you know about the contributions they've made to the field of storytelling the more colors you have available to you to paint the subtle contours of the potential stories in front of you. Through hard work (and a ton of luck) I've found a way to straddle different perspectives on stories, which is something that being in between cultures and always keeping an open mind has allowed me to do. That is the lens through which I wrote this book and I hope that what I'm proposing to you becomes all the more valuable because of it.

There have been several excellent books that have enriched readers' understanding of storytelling and the role that stories play in business contexts. Books like *Story* (McKee) and *Story Trumps Structure* (James) are immeasurably instructive when it comes to understanding the fundamentals of story building. Titles like *Wired for Story* (Cron) and *The Story Factor* (Simmons) integrate story structure with studies that show how the brain responds to ideas that have been crafted in a certain way. And bestsellers like *Stories at Work* (Chakraborty) and *How to Talk like TED* (Gallo) have been indispensable in taking these insights and putting them to work for professionals in order to improve messaging in organizations. My book seeks to take cues from many of these but also to contribute something new. Specifically, this book proposes that common misunderstandings regarding stories have diluted the potential that storytelling actually has. Because of this, my goal is to acquaint the reader with the nuts and bolts of story structure across contexts and genres, and then to take that skill set and apply it to the eight situations where adapted versions of that structure will prove immediately effective.

As for what follows, the book is divided into four sections. First, I discuss why asking some fundamental questions about what stories are (and aren't) is so important. Here, I expand on misnomers and misperceptions about stories. I also lay out the case for using correct terminology. Why? Because I believe that clear verbal labeling leads to lucid idea construction. Next, in perhaps the most important section, I get very specific about story construction and the theoretical and practical underpinnings of the universal story structure. Here in Part 2, I describe The Base, one of the eight stories this book proposes and the most important one since it serves as the template off of which all seven of the remaining stories will be built. Part 3 looks closely at each of those seven stories and how they both compare and contrast with The Base. And lastly, in Part 4, I discuss the challenges surrounding harvesting stories, or finding and nurturing the stories inside and around us. It's one thing to understand how a bridge is constructed. And yet it's another thing to source the best possible materials for the job. Thankfully, training yourself and others to be better at looking for, and discovering, source material for your stories is something that can be learned. Adding this final piece of the puzzle means never running out of stories and always finding a way to retrieve and catalog the highlights of our lives.

I'm very excited to be taking this journey with you. Yes, this book is meant to educate and explain what I think is a critical concept that will make an immediate difference in your presentations, writing, and brand projection. But I also believe that if you read this with an open mind and a willingness to experiment, you won't be able to help but start to accumulate your own stories as you go along. So pair this text with a notebook and make your experience here more than just passive intake. Make it an excuse to journal. Make it a reason to explore your world a little deeper. And make it an opportunity to transform your own storytelling skills in ways that you might not have ever predicted. I won't be telling you that "you need" to do this or that like, sadly, many other authors do. Find what works for you and what doesn't work (which is actually even more important) and use this book a set of principles and observations to help light the way.

And lastly, I think it's extremely important to keep in mind that storytelling is not a magical fix. There are countless situations where a story is *not* the right choice as the centerpiece of a presentation. For earnings reports, progress reviews, quality control assessments, or interviews (to name just a few) using stories would often be confusing and even obfuscatory, not to mention unprofessional. As a communications mantra, "when in doubt, use a story" is a terrible idea. Any presentation that you put together is most likely to have some story elements and some non-story elements. But when a situation arises where you have more time, where context and background are important, and where the way that change happened in your own life, in your company's history, or in another organization's past can serve to instruct and inspire, stories can do wonders. And when that happens, the eight simple to understand tracks presented here provide eight avenues towards success that, once mastered, you will use over and over again.

CHAPTER 1 – DEFINITIONS AND CONTOURS

The Unavoidable Question

Before we can move into The Base, the story format that essentially serves as the template for the other seven story types this book proposes, there is one simple question that can't be avoided: What is a story? You might think that this question is either too basic or unnecessary. But in fact, it's anything but basic and it's absolutely critical. Allow me to explain why.

I like to go to writing workshops myself. I have been to perhaps fifty of them over the years and I would say half of them have been helpful in introducing me to a detail I hadn't considered fully while half of them were built on general cheerleading mixed with a fair share of clichés. Several years ago I was in a workshop and, in all honesty, I wasn't feeling it. I would never suggest that the

10

workshop wasn't at my "level" a) because I don't really believe in levels; and b) because I think it's so important to keep returning to foundational elements in writing over and over. It was more like the workshop wasn't providing concrete advice that I could use. Just then, a young man in front of me put his hand up and the facilitator called on him. He said, "I know this is a really stupid question, but I just thought I'd ask it before we went any further. What exactly *is* a story?" Suddenly, I became very interested. I love this question and I was extremely curious about how the teacher was going to answer. And she said, "Oh, thanks for the question. That's very easy. A story is something with a beginning, middle, and end." I sighed. Yes, that's true but a football match also has a beginning, middle, and end. So does a tornado, a kidney stone, or breakfast.

But to let the teacher off the hook for a second, in the twenty-first century, more so than at any time before, the word "story" isn't easy to define. Newspaper reporters are filing stories, George R. R. Martin is writing stories 1000 pages long, some people are suggesting that you can compose stories in 140 characters, TV anchors are narrating stories, forensic scientists say the evidence tells a story, while Instagram says that your morning Zumba class is also a story. It's getting to the point where any pile of words or any moment that you can think of is a "story."

In fact, I would go so far as to say that the word story is one of the most overused words in the English language. It's not even really a word at this point, but an umbrella concept that covers all kinds of components that have one thing in common: "things I find interesting." In other words, it's a word that has been pulled and stretched and morphed into anything we want it to mean. The only word in English that comes to mind for me that's treated equally as vaguely is the word "democracy." Democracy has basically come to mean any group, organization, or country that has voting. But all it takes is about five seconds to realize that that makes no sense. I mean, *North Korea* has voting. Democracy is made up of preconditions without which the term is meaningless: ideas like human rights, gender equality, workers' protections, freedom of speech, the ability to assemble, and so on. These are so fundamental that they cannot be separated from any reasonable use of the word democracy. Nevertheless, it's become a placeholder, a catch-all term, a word that "everyone knows" therefore there's no need to define it. The same is true of the word story.

When I discuss this point in my workshop I start to get several furrowed brows in the audience. People like the ring of "everything is a story" or "every moment is a story" and they're protective of it. I'll admit, it's a very pleasant-sounding thing. It gives us a magical feeling of unity when we hear it. So the participants with worried looks on their faces will ask, "Can't we just take a wider approach to the word? Why do you have to try to burst everyone's bubble and pin in down?"

Here's why. Let's say that you want to be better at repairing helicopters. And in addition to that, you don't like how people divide transportation devices into so many different categories: escalators, cars, trucks, boats, jets, hovercrafts, hang gliders, and so on. And so you decide to call everything a helicopter no matter what it is. Sure you can do that. However, when it comes time for you to learn more about how to repair helicopters, you're going to run into a problem very quickly. Not only that, but you're going to spend a lot of time looking at things that are outside of the scope of what you're trying to learn. In other words, if everything is a helicopter, then what is the likelihood that you'll find a way to truly address the needs you have about how to build them? Will you discover the information you're after? If this metaphor doesn't resonate with you, just ask a legal prosecutor how airtight her case would be if she didn't bother to define the criminal charges against the defendant and whether they matched the actions that he took. She can't get away with avoiding defining those charges. In fact, defining the charges is the doorway that opens up the entire investigation exercise.

In other words, in order to study anything we must always begin with defining the object under investigation. This is not optional and it's not avoidable even if doing so doesn't seem very "nice." This is obvious when you apply it to any other field of study. But when you do it with stories, you're messing with something that people cherish, an indescribable elusiveness that they've embraced. This just demonstrates how overused this word has become.

Baby Steps

Because the word comes with so much baggage, I think it's fair to say that proposing a specific way of looking at what a story is need not be rushed. So let's not do that. Let's take our time and take small steps towards an answer, signposting some important insights along the way.

Like other scholars of storytelling often suggest, I would argue that you already know how to tell a story. Perhaps not consciously, but subconsciously. That's because storytelling is in your DNA. When I say that, don't get me wrong. Many people use the phrase "in your DNA" as a fancy sounding substitute for someone being good at something—like tennis is in Steffi Graf's DNA or painting was in Francisco Goya's DNA. I don't mean it like that. I mean literally that storytelling is part of your genetic code.

The first hint that this might be true involves looking closely at what we're good at as a species. You don't have to be an evolutionary biologist to notice that human beings aren't particularly good at most things. We can't run very fast. We can't jump very far. We can't carry very much weight. And we can't climb very quickly. But we seem to be able to do things with our brains that other creatures can't do. I like to call them mental acrobatics. We can think of hundreds of examples but one of my favorites is that we're probably the only species that can entertain the possibility that we might not exist. (I'm a huge fan of dolphins and maybe someday we'll discover that dolphins too are capable of an existential crisis, but for the moment it seems like there are certain acrobatics that are exclusive to us.) We can arrange ideas and suspend our perception of reality while bending it and questioning it.

I would go so far as to suggest that storytelling is our species' superpower. Neurological studies have confirmed that regions of the brain light up when a person hears a story and that the body produces chemicals specifically in response to story input. There is something unique about stories and our species. You don't need to tell a cheetah how to run. You don't need to tell a peregrine falcon how to fly. And you don't need to tell a human being how to tell a story. It's in your bones already. But like a caged cheetah or falcon we haven't been fully acquainted with what we're capable of. Let's push this concept further and get more specific.

So yes, we seem to be able to do things with our brains that only our species can probably do, but still, is storytelling really in our DNA? Yes. And the hint to the answer as to why is to ask yourself why anything is in any creature's DNA. After all these millions of years of life on this planet, why have some strands of specific biological coding been passed down to various creatures all the way to the present day? Because those specific traits had some role to play in their survival. This observation was as true in Darwin's study of Galapagos Island birds in the 1850s as it is today. And of course it leads to the obvious question: but what does storytelling have to do with our survival?

Our ancestors had many things to worry about. They had to reliably find food, water, shelter, safety from predators, and escape from harsh natural elements. They had communication but they didn't have the benefit of writing. So they could only share orally. Their breakthroughs and realizations needed recognition so that everyone in their clan could benefit from them. But it wasn't just their immediate group that they hoped to share major insights with, but eventually their children's group, and their children's children's group, and so on. And so, and I think this is best articulated by author and storyteller Doug Lipman, our ancestors on the African savanna invented a *technology* that would allow them to not only assemble information, but to assemble it in a way that would outlive them. To put it simply, they found a way to assemble information to ensure that it would never be forgotten.

And that's our first definition of what a story is: a story is information that has been packaged in a particular way to make it unforgettable.

But what *is* that package? Let's keep going.

There are three quotes that directly or indirectly propose definitions of what a story is that l like to keep handy because they each say something unique for me and help to take the ideas we've just been entertaining to the next level. The first one is this, from Spanish novelist Carlos Ruiz Zafón:

"A story is a letter that the author writes to herself to tell herself things that she would otherwise be unable to discover."

I love that definition so much. It reminds me of the important mantra, "Enjoy the journey, not just the destination." It suggests that a story is not like taking out a treasure map, taking ten paces towards a giant X, and then digging up your story to share with the world. It's more like an adventure where you're headed one place only to realize that the real story is lurking somewhere hidden around the corner. I think this is profoundly important because even though storytelling is our superpower, protecting ourselves is also a major psychological priority. And very often when we seem to have discovered a story, especially one about our own lives, it's more like we've opened the first door to a house and are standing in the foyer. But the real story, the story that the foyer is only hinting it, is four rooms deep into the house. The reason we don't automatically go straight to where the real story lives is because something else also lives there in the center of the house: trauma, pain, and other things that we don't want to look at. Many storytellers don't realize at first that these rooms are where the most important stories are. So being a storyteller takes courage. Thankfully, the more you practice this the less likely you'll be to stop at the foyer.

Another definition comes from the *Cambridge Dictionary Online*. It says that a story is the following:

"a description, either true or imagined, of a connected series of events"

Not quite as poetic as Zafón's quote but important nonetheless. In fact, there's one word in that definition that's critical and we will come to it in the pages ahead.

Lastly, there's this definition from storytelling researcher Pamela Rutledge:

"Stories are how we think. They are how we make meaning of life. Call them schema, scripts, cognitive maps, mental models, metaphors, or narratives. Stories are how we explain how things work, how we make decisions, how we justify our decisions, how we persuade others, how we understand our place in the world, create our identities, and define and teach social values."

Even now, after sharing this quote hundreds of times in my workshops, as I write this, I still shake my head and laugh a little because of my background. I did my Ph.D. on storytelling in documentary film history and in one of the sections of my writing I looked at the psychological pitfalls of storytelling, the dark underside where inspiration meets coercion, and where role modeling meets manipulation. In those days I would snicker at any definition that suggested storytelling was so important. But in the decades that have passed since then, I've changed. While I still firmly believe in the dark underside of oppression dressed as storytelling, I also believe that stories, as the definition implies, are the filters through which we experience the world, how we make sense out of it, remember it, and, maybe more importantly, find meaning in it.

Let's look at a different quote that I think helps push us forward just a little bit more when it comes to defining what a story is. Best-selling author and TED speaker Brené Brown suggested that, "Maybe stories are just data with a soul." There's something that I really like about this quote (perhaps that it packs a punch in so few words) but also something that I'm not so crazy about. If we think about this as a mathematical equation for a second, we get "stories = data + soul." That seems like a fair way to rewrite Brown's quote.

The part that I like is that she proposes that a story is more than data—facts, figures, dates, numbers, etc. The part that I don't like is the word "soul." It means something different to everyone. Maybe that's the exact reason why the quote has gotten so much traction. But that very factor makes it slightly less useful for us if our goal is an objective, rather than subjective, investigation into exactly what a story is.

You might be saying to yourself, *Yes, well, of course stories are more than information. A lot more.* But, remember what we said earlier about the word "story" and how it's treated? What might appear obvious to you now that you're looking at what a story is under a magnifying glass, is not obvious to most people right away. I know this because of the volume of material that I've had submitted to me both as a writing coach and as the curator of the live storytelling performances that we organize at Tall Tales.

Because of the way we ask for stories and because of the reputation of the kinds of stories that we spotlight in our collection, things have gotten better, but there are still massive amounts of non-stories that are sent my way. For all intents and purposes these non-story submissions could be called, "My Crazy Beach Weekend." And inside we read about this thing that happened, then that thing that happened, then this next shocking thing that happened, and then this funny thing that happened, and so on. Objectively analyzing the piece, what is it? What is it really? It's actually just a list of things that happened. And it's about as interesting as your daily to-do list. In other words, it's just information. I can't tell you how many times I have written in the margins of aspiring writers' work something like, "This is just stuff happening." In the pages ahead we'll learn more about why "stuff happening" isn't enough, but at this point, the reason that it falls short is because it's just a string of events in a list. Is it important? Absolutely. Is the skeleton an important part of the body? For sure. But is the skeleton enough? No. We need something else to make a list, an amalgamation of information, into something more.

Three Terms

Another way of thinking about this idea is by looking at three common terms and how (or whether) they're connected. Let's start with the first two: information and knowledge. I want you to take a 30-second break from this book and to think about the difference between these two words? Maybe there isn't a difference. If you feel like there is one, what is it? How would you articulate it?

I don't think there are any wrong answers to this but the answer that I find most satisfying is that information is data, like names and dates and numbers, while knowledge is taking that data and attempting to achieve something larger with it, a process that might very likely involve selecting and not selecting certain pieces of information to accomplish a larger goal. So information is all the ingredients in your kitchen. Knowledge is selecting and combining certain ones to make pancakes. Information is all the different parts of a parachute. Knowledge is deciding which of those pieces come into play at specific times in order for you to successfully skydive.

Let's add one more word into the mix: wisdom. Where does this word fit with the other two? Again, no wrong answers, but perhaps the most common suggestion that I hear in my workshops is that wisdom is what you get when you extend knowledge over time. In other words, gaining knowledge over and over and over again eventually gets you to wisdom. There's nothing wrong with that suggestion at all and it rings true to me. But the one that's most satisfying to me is that wisdom is the moral dimension of knowledge.

So let's take an example. I'm writing this chapter from my living room apartment in Pune, India right now. If I somehow had an atomic bomb in here and I took it completely apart and laid out every piece on the floor—every metal casing, screw, spring, wire, and ounce of uranium—and labeled each piece, which of our three terms would that represent? Information. Now, if I took those pieces and assembled them together in order to achieve something larger, which term does that correspond to? Knowledge. Now that this thing is assembled, there's a looming question of whether it is ever morally acceptable to use such a device. That's wisdom. So I would say that wisdom is the moral or ethical dimension of knowledge. Stories start in the realm of information but eventually come to live in the nexus between knowledge and wisdom.

Not Quite a Story

Let's look at another term that introduces something very important as we move closer and closer to a definition of what a story is: anecdote. What is an anecdote? Most people believe that an anecdote is a personal story, but that's not quite accurate. An anecdote is a short recounting of an incident that will often either have a funny ending or a lesson embedded in its conclusion. You can also say that many anecdotes are examples or illustrations of an idea, a confirmation that some idea is indeed valid. With the all-encompassing way that stories are defined in pop culture, anecdotes are often called stories—but not by me here. Our job here is to sift through the misnomers and find out what story actually is. So, if anecdotes are not stories then what's the difference between them? The answer has to do with the hint from the dictionary several pages ago. The dictionary definition proposed the word "series"—and that's the key. An anecdote is a single incident while a story is multiple incidents. Again, you're likely saying to yourself that this is obvious. But, this seemingly small detail has wide-ranging implications.

Having multiple incidents allows something to happen that a single incident doesn't allow. You could say it gives birth to, or makes possible, an observation that was not possible before. And it's so important that it's the centerpiece of another handy definition of what a story is:

A story is a vehicle for change.

In other words, a story is a "stage" that allows change to take place. Single incidents are single snapshots in time. We can speculate about how things got to that point but in the end they are frozen moments, isolated from context. Multiple incidents are at least two snapshots in time. When we have more than one snapshot we can compare and contrast the two. What are the similarities between them, and, crucially, what are the differences? When we have the movement from one state to another state then we have change. And when we have change we have the most important characteristic of a story. Change must be present or there is no story. Again, I know this is sometimes hard to hear in our current age, but change must be present.

To qualify as a story, there must be change. And when thinking about change, you can think about the Big Three. The Big Three are the three most common categories of change. They are so common that they are likely present in any story that you can remember whether it's written, oral, or visual. The first is change in circumstance. So the city is in fear of government surveillance at the beginning of the story, the city is free from government surveillance at the end. Or the billiards player is a novice at the beginning of the story, he's an expert hustler by the end. The second category is change in insight. So the main character is trying to be the perfect daughter at the beginning of the story, and by the end realizes that this is not possible and she must try to only do her best. The newly incarcerated prisoner is a rudderless youth destined for a life of crime at the beginning of the story, and after given direction and inspiration becomes a highly educated and powerful civil rights leader by the end. And the third category is change in relationship. Two people are strangers at the beginning of the story, and those people are lovers at the end. Those are the

Big Three: changes in the world, changes inside the mind of the main character, and changes in the relationship between the main character and someone else. Most stories, even short stories, will contain more than one of these changes, but technically speaking, as long as one is present, we're still in the realm of storytelling.

To cap off this section it's worth adding one more element to the discussion. This book is not a workbook or a duplication of my workshop, but I'll explain what we do in my live workshop at this particular moment following the introduction of change. If we think about the metaphor of a story kind of being like an adult (and granted we do not yet know exactly what a story is), we can think of anecdotes as kind of like adolescents. By growing an anecdote, by adding multiple anecdotes, multiple incidents together, we can reach an adult, a story. Well, let's take the metaphor back to its logical beginning. What do stories look like when they're born? The concept that I discovered in *Measures of a Story* by K. Sean Buvala and that I've found incredibly useful in my work, is something called a "float."

A float is a single sentence that is entirely subjective. A float can be a memory, a passion, a love, a hate, or a specific, personal observation. The key is that it's subjective. So, let's look at some examples. "I'm terrified of the ocean." Is this a float? Yes. It immediately gets you wondering why. What happened to you to make you so scared of the ocean? "The most important night of my life was October 17th, 1979." Is this a float? Yes. It's a specific memory and it also prompts the question of why. What about, "I love chocolate cake" as a float? Does it qualify? Yes, it is, but we're also now seeing the difference between more interesting floats and less interesting ones. The reason that this one is less intriguing is because the in-group is so large. In other words, the number of people who love chocolate cake is so high that it borders on objectivity. Speaking of that, what about this one? "The sky is blue." Is this a float? No. It's an objective observation.

Floats are incredibly useful to design because they focus on what makes you (or if you're writing fiction, your *character*) unique. They are story seeds that you unpack and extrapolate from. Why did this float come about and how did things develop afterwards? Just like an actual seed, the float contains all the elements for the story to come. But, and this is critical, just like an actual oak tree seed, a float doesn't look like a mini-oak tree. It looks quite different. This is extremely important because, as the letter-writing definition we opened with suggested, we must always stay aware of the fact that the story might unravel itself very differently than we first anticipate. In fact, though I love floats and find them to be excellent ways to start if you're feeling stuck, I always tell people I work with to not get "married" to their floats. What I mean by that is that sometimes the destiny of a float is for it to be ultimately discarded in favor of the real float that was hiding under the surface that only became visible with some mental unpacking.

I hope that some floats are now bouncing around in your head. If they are, write them down. The purpose of this book is not only to provide you a roadmap for how to tell eight business stories but to get you thinking about the experiences that shaped your personal history and work life the most. Now is a good time to pay attention to the voices inside you. Maybe there's a story that's been dying to be told for a very long time but you've never given yourself the excuse to put it into words. Try writing five floats and see how it goes. Keep them. Set them aside. You might very well want to plant them in the future.

The more overtly philosophical section of this book is now over. But I think it's crucial. If indeed the word story is one of the most overused words, then any larger discussion that puts stories at the center must do some groundwork to make sure that concepts and definitions are clear. There is no need to agree with me of course. But at least you know what I believe and why I believe it. I always joke with those I work with by telling them that after our class (or after you finish this book) you can go back to using the word "story" however you like, but while we're partners in this investigation, we're looking at this word not only under a magnifying glass but under a microscope, and we need to correspondingly tighten our definition. When we do that, details that were once fuzzy can suddenly become self-evident. And the discussion that follows becomes all more fruitful because of it.

CHAPTER 2 – THE USS AND THE BASE

The Ghost in the Machine

I'll now get a lot more practical in answering the question of what a story is. This section details the universal story structure, the pattern noticeable in any memorable story. The stories that stick with us, the stories that move us, the stories that inspire us, and the stories that change the course of our lives have something in common: this structure. It's called the universal story structure because my proposal is that if a piece of writing does not have these elements then it's not a story. In other words, if this structure is not present, there is no point in kidding ourselves: we haven't reached the realm of storytelling yet. It's like asking if a pile of bricks is the same as a house. Well, no. That pile has the *potential* to become a house but those bricks must be assembled in a certain way. Same exact idea here.

As the overarching purpose of this book is to introduce eight story formats, the universal story structure is also the structure of The Base. The Base is the most important of all eight of the story formats covered in this book. It's the core structure that the other seven stories are modified versions of. The Base could have also been called the personal story. The personal story (or first-person narrative) presents a slice of life that centers on a change in circumstance, insight, and/or relationship. It can be funny, instructive, dramatic and/or everything in between. The Base is an incredibly useful story to tell in a massively wide range of contexts. I will mention some at the end of this subsection.

This next point is borderline obvious but you'll see later why I'm mentioning it here. This is the universal story structure for fiction *and nonfiction* stories. So stories from your imagination as well as stories from real life. Those who embrace the idea that "everything is a story" will especially buckle at this declaration, but it's true. We do not need to create one pattern for make-believe and one pattern for the world we live in. If we assemble a pile of bricks into a house in the real world, we have rules and boundaries like size, budget, and gravity. If we write a fictional story about doing so, then we also have to follow those rules of reality. If we build one in a galaxy far, far away where those rules no longer apply, then we create new rules for that place and our imaginary designs must abide by *those* rules. Story structure spans and outlines the borders of worlds we know as well as ones we create. More on this later.

I want to summarize what The Base actually is one more time because this point is so foundational for the rest of the book. I believe that the universal story structure is the structure for any memorable story. It also is, simultaneously, the structure of The Base, the core story off of which all the other stories in this book are based. In other words, once you've mastered The Base, you are now 80% of the way towards being able to build and tell any story that you need to. The rest of this book will teach you how to adapt and modify that core story in seven different ways.

Let's talk for a moment about writing, because writing is not exactly the same as storytelling and if you don't write, you might be worried about how many times I've mentioned writing so far. I sometimes hear from people who say to me that after looking closely, they realized that my class, book, or workshop wasn't for them because they deliver stories (or presentations that center on stories) orally and not in written form, and my work focuses more on the written form. This is incorrect or, perhaps more accurately, drastically incomplete. Let's go back to the house metaphor. Imagine that you hired someone to build a house for you and the architect showed up with nothing—no supplies, no plans, no drawings. You'd ask her where the blueprints are. What if she said to you that she's really not into writing things down but would rather hold it all in her head? I think in that case it would be time to find a new architect. The same thing holds for story design. No matter what the final delivery mechanism is for a story—on paper, on a screen, into a microphone, or something else—any worthwhile work starts on paper with writing. Writing provides a mental workshop, a canvas, where you can test ideas, move them around, make mistakes, and find the order, connections, and transitions that are most effective. You do not need to be a Pulitzer Prize-winning author to write. Anyone who is trying to organize their ideas can and should be writing.

And one final note before we detail the pattern that unifies all memorable stories. There is a misinterpretation about my concentration on the universal story structure that is common enough that I want to address it here. Some people detect an implication that what I'm saying here is that if something is a story then you've got something worthwhile and if you have something that falls short of a story then you have something inferior. Another way of putting this is that by highlighting story structure, I'm indirectly suggesting that anything outside of this structure doesn't matter. This could not be further from the truth. Instead, what I am saying here is that this pattern is the pattern for perception-changing, cathartic, powerful, and most importantly, memorable storytelling. If a piece of writing does not fit into this pattern, it may still be incredible in its own way: it's just not a story. For example, it might be a poem. Or a sentence or two that gets you to think. Or a stream of consciousness that gives a peak into someone else's point of view. Let's let these things be what they are. They do not *have* to be stories. They are wonderful in their own right. It's not only incorrect, but actually unfair to call them stories. Let them be what they are and still be magical. Some of my favorite things ever written are not stories. I cherish them. I also recognize that at the same time for something to in fact be a story, there are certain characteristics that we're looking for. What those are, in detail, is what follows now.

The Arc

There are countless ways that the universal story structure can be presented. I could just present a list of elements and characteristics and then describe them. But I believe strongly in taking the best of the ideas that have come before us and using them to our advantage. With this in mind, I find the Story Arc (otherwise known as the Narrative Arc or Freytag's Pyramid) to be a helpful visual reinforcement of the ideas that I'll be discussing. My proposal is that there are 4.5 sections of this arc, so 4.5 elements of the universal story structure, some of which have extensive sub-elements. And, just to reiterate one final time, these elements are not just important but universal in my mind because if any of these elements or sub-elements are missing, then we have something other than a story. When all of these elements and sub-elements are in place, then we have the sound, fundamental structural underpinnings of a story and can move onto other considerations such as how to make it especially captivating, how to give it depth, and how to avoid common mistakes that many storytellers make.

THE ARC

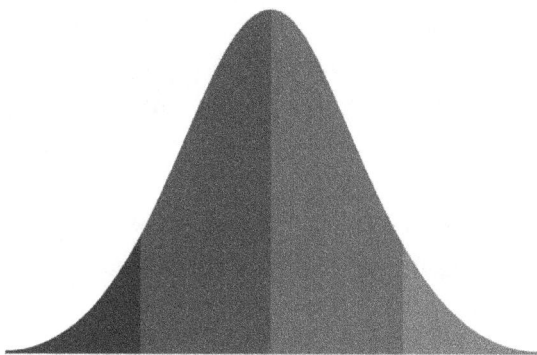

Exposition

Exposition is the first universal story structure element that I will discuss, moving from left to right on the arc diagram. Exposition means the "who," "what," "where," and "when" of the story. The "who" refers to the character (or characters) in a story. The "what" refers to what does the main character want the most. The "where" refers to the location/s where the story takes place. And the "when" refers to the time-period or duration frame of the story. Perhaps you've come across other advice at some point in your story studies that used a different term than the word exposition. For example, you often hear the word "setting" used in describing the first consideration in story building. There's nothing wrong with that, but for me personally, when I think of setting my mind immediately jumps to "where" alone; but what's needed is more than just the "where." We need all four of the sub-elements above. The word exposition explicitly covers those four sub-elements and so for me it's a more useful term than setting or context or something else along those lines.

If you've ever taken a journalism class or have worked for a news outlet of any kind, chances are very high that you've heard that there are six question words that should be addressed as early as possible in reporting. Looking back at our four words above, we can see that two of these six words are missing: "why" and "how." Those are missing because, to put it simply, that's the *story* part. The exposition is like building the foundation of a house and answering the why and how is the rest of the house on top of that.

The exposition's central purpose is to introduce the four sub-elements and by doing so, to establish the normal routine, or everyday world of the story. By far, the best way to wrap your mind around this is to look at any fairytale. All fairytales start with something like what follows (I have put exposition elements in parentheses):

Once upon a time (when) there was a castle (where) and in that castle lived two princesses (who) who cared for the local village's animals more than anything in the world (what).

We can see that in one sentence all the pieces have been included. The single-sentence format rarely happens outside of the world of fairytales, but it's still useful to see how these iconic opening lines check all of the needed boxes.

After a few minutes of thinking about it, you quickly see that exposition is important but that the real challenge is not simply providing exposition but in deciding *how* to provide it. In other words, exposition delivery is an entire topic onto itself. There are many ways that exposition can be delivered in a story, but from 35,000 feet looking down, if you could sort all storytelling into categories of exposition delivery, you would notice three patterns: expositions that are delivered upfront, little by little, and at the end. So let's take these one at a time, but let's recognize one crucial caveat first. Exposition is being delivered all throughout a story. After all, new characters are being introduced all the time and new locations are being travelled to. So all stories, for the most part, have a current running under them that we could call the exposition. However, what the three categories represent are extra doses of exposition being delivered at certain times. I like to think of it as if sugar is being sprinkled on a story all the way through, but with upfront exposition delivery we're adding extra sugar at the beginning, with little by little deliberate doses at particular times, and then with backloaded, an extra dose at the end. Again, sprinkling is always happening but there are noticeable patterns where it's happening a little more or a little less in certain places.

Upfront exposition delivery refers to providing extra exposition at the beginning. Sometimes, when I'm working with writers I will ask questions about the exposition like, "I'm a bit confused by the choice of exposition delivery method that you opted for." And I will get answers like, "Well, that's my style of storytelling." I often ask in response, "But what is the *story* asking you to do?" In other words, sometimes the particulars of the story itself call for certain types of exposition delivery. These are not entirely arbitrary decisions on the part of the storyteller. There are two central conditions that call for an upfront delivery. The mental checklist is whether a story's exposition is unusual or complicated. If a story's exposition is either unusual or complicated then we will need an extra dose of exposition at the start. What kinds of stories nearly always fall into those categories? Science fiction and fantasy. But even beyond those, we can think of countless practical examples from our own time and universe: introducing the exposition of someone who specializes in saving the lives of crewmen trapped on submarines; laying out the routine of a dealer who specializes in black market goods; building the normal, everyday world of the lead researcher on the International Space Station studying the effects of anti-gravity on bacterial growth. We could think of hundreds more if we took the time. Because these expositions require more world-building than more usual expositions, the reader or audience needs that extra background at the start (or very close to the start) in order to be able to follow the story. In science fiction and fantasy literature we often see things like maps right in the first few pages, pointing out the shape, contours, and borders of the world where the story takes place. What is that? It's actually a very explicit form of upfront exposition.

The second category is little by little. This one is, I think, the hardest to wrap your mind around simply because, as I stated in the above caveat, *all* story expositions are really little by little. For this style, we should be thinking about stories that, in addition to sprinkling exposition all throughout, also add deliberate larger doses at certain junctures. The kind of storytelling that calls for this style is episodic storytelling. Episodic storytelling means introducing a set of who, what, where, and when in one place and then moving over to introduce an entirely new set in another place, and then doing it again and so on, returning back and forth between them to move the meta-story forward. To use a recent well-known example, we can think of *Game of Thrones*. We're going to introduce one set of people in this part of Westeros and then move over to another part and another entirely different set of people and relationships and then cut back and forth. Imagine a business-related story that takes place in three countries with three separate businesses. Same idea would apply.

The final delivery style is backloaded, where extra exposition is given at the end. The simple term for this is a twist. A twist is when the reader or audience is given information about an aspect of who, what, where, or when that could have been given at the beginning of a story but was saved for the end, forcing the receiver to reevaluate everything that happened previously with this new realization in hand. In the mystery genre, often a detective archetype will, at the end of the story, piece together details from the beginning providing new insight and interpretation that saves the day and catches the bad guy. For the personal story, especially the nonfiction personal story, the storyteller himself will share a new insight or detail that he in fact actually learned late in the story as the backloaded exposition.

One of my favorite additional definitions of exposition is that exposition is what happens before the story starts. Another term for that is background or context: the pieces that you need to know in order for the story to begin. I like to think of the exposition as not the story itself *per se* but rather the cup or bowl that the story is poured into. A bowl provides the locale and the boundaries of something that's going to be inside of it. Likewise, the exposition frames the story while announcing its principle players.

So since I'm talking about required elements of a story now, and not "things that you should consider to make your story more interesting," we should ask if you really do in fact need exposition. The answer is yes. Because without characters, what's driving them, an initial location, and a time period, it will be very difficult to have anything that even resembles a story. But let's push this idea to its limit. If the exposition of a story is like the foundation of a house, it's logical to ask this: can you build a house without a foundation? The answer is surprisingly yes. Of course you can. But what are the consequences of that?

Without a foundation, the likelihood that the house will be able to stand for any significant length of time is greatly diminished. The storytelling equivalent of that is that the reader puts down your story or the audience in the room tunes out. We often hear people say (and we often say ourselves) that a story didn't "grab" them or that they "just couldn't get into it." Very often, the reason this happens is because there is some critical flaw in the exposition or the exposition delivery method. If the reader feels consistently disoriented, her patience will wear thin and eventually she'll give up. Maybe you were looking forward to knocking her socks off with the amazing ending that's coming, but she's abandoned the story way before that because of structural flaws. Therefore, exposition delivery is just as critical a consideration as exposition itself.

To summarize, exposition is the who, what, where, and when of a story. I touched on all of these above but spent less time looking closely at the "what," which refers to what the main character wants the most. That's because this element is more complicated than it might seem at first and so I'll save that for a little later in this book. But the other pieces should be very clear. Exposition is kind of like setting up a chessboard. We put all the pieces in the squares where they go. We note the boundaries of the game board. And we recognize that the pieces have various characteristics and move in certain ways depending on their roles. But all of that, looking at it from a blueprint perspective, is just preparation. Once that's done it's time to start the game. And that's the next element.

EXPOSITION

The who, what, where, and when of the story

The foundation of the house that grounds and orients the reader or audience

The exposition is what happens before the story starts. It establishes the normal, routine world for the characters. While it is a part of the universal story structure, it can also be thought of as the "cup" that the story is poured into.

Action

While action is the second element of the universal story structure, it's not enough to simply check off the "stuff happened" box. What *exactly* is happening? But more importantly, how do those pieces of what's happening link to each other over time? This last question is so crucial. These elements and sub-elements are not being included for some arbitrary or cosmetic reason. Like the inner-workings of a watch, each piece is there because it serves a function and is connected to another piece doing something connected to another piece. Remove a gear of the watch and the watch stops. Remove an element of the universal story structure and the story doesn't make sense.

The action section of the story arc might represent over 90% of the length of the entire story. This is for reasons I'll discuss later. Because of this, there are eight identifiable subsections of the action section, each playing a critical role. To articulate these sections I will be using my own notes, research, and observations but I will also be leaning on two of my favorite story structure resources: *The Hero of a Thousand Faces*, the seminal book by the late world-renowned comparative mythologist Joseph Campbell as well as writer John Yorke's text on the five act story structure, *Into the Woods*. Campbell is more useful in some of the earlier subsections while Yorke is germane in the latter ones.

Inciting Incident

As I mentioned above, we all know the first line of any fairytale. But what's the first line on page 2? If you think about it for a second, you'll realize that it's, "But one day…" The routine, normal world was established at the outset and then the routine was broken. The term for that is inciting incident. It may be useful here at this point to address a question that might be starting to form in the back of your mind. Your question might be something like this: "Are we talking about the *order* in which these things happen in a story? After all, most stories don't follow the fairytale pattern, correct?" Correct. We are not talking about the order in which the elements tend to appear. Outside of children's stories the elements very rarely appear in the exact order that we're going to introduce them, but we have to introduce them in *some* order, so I'm choosing to make my way, left to right, so to speak, across the arc. Just to cap this point, and the reason why I'm mentioning this right at this moment, is that the inciting incident is very often the place that a story will actually start, whether it's on paper, on a screen, or somewhere else. Very often a routine is broken and then *later on* we find out exactly what that routine was.

One quick note about the word "hero." I will often be using this word in the continuing discussion. Consider this word interchangeable with main character, keeping in mind that the main character may very well be you. This is important because I don't want you to fixate on a muscle-bound demigod or someone with superpowers when you read that word. I just want you to think of the main character. This may be a fictional character of course, but since the trajectory of this book will eventually lead us to a broader picture of the business storytelling landscape, think of the hero as yourself or another person whose nonfiction story is being designed.

The Revelation

If you had to select the most important of all the large or small elements of the universal story structure, it could easily be argued that the revelation is either the most important or the second most important of them all. This is because the revelation does three critical things in a story that have wide ramifications.

First, it confirms that the break in routine is significant. If you look very closely at a story you might find things that appear to be small breaks in routine—a teenager tends to order a latte every morning at a coffee shop but this one day orders an espresso. Is it important? Probably not. But the revelation is going to let us know. A factory worker comes to work everyday but one day is furloughed. Is it important? Very likely. But the revelation is going to let us know. Second, the revelation introduces the problem of the story. Every story has a problem of some kind, most often the problem of how to obtain something or how to protect against something. Just like the change-related definition of what a story was that I mentioned earlier, you could also argue that, simply put, a story is an attempt to solve a problem. And third, the revelation sets two or more forces into motion that are trying to solve that problem in their own favor. This is the introduction of the conflict. More about these later, but for now, let's look at an example to see these in action. I have added notations above the section that describes the sections below each of them.

[exposition]

Our story opens on a researcher in a Northern California university astronomy center. She's a professor of astrophysics and oversees operation of the school's state-of-the-art deep-space telescope. After pouring herself a cup of coffee, she makes her way through the corridor until she reaches the telescope's base and the semi-circular lab around it. She flips on a few switches, glances at the logout book from the night before, and moves over to do a quick check-in with what she was working on before she left the previous day. She takes a look at her notes and then takes a look at the three photos that she asked one of her graduate students to take during the night. She looks confused—and spills a little coffee.

[break in routine]

She looks back at her notes. Back to the photo. Then opens up some raw data on the computer. Then she looks back at the notes. She knows it's only 7:30 am but she calls two of her graduate students anyway and asks them a few questions that they can't answer without being in the lab, so they come in. All of them are looking at the readouts together and the professor says, "This doesn't make any sense. Have you seen anything like this before?" The students all shake their heads no.

[significance of break in routine]

They discuss the details of these readings and how the cluster of objects they've been studying in the sky didn't behave according to the predictive models that they had created. If these photos are accurate then the cosmic objects are not what they thought they were. In fact, they're acting like meteors in between our solar system and that of one of our neighbors.

[problem of the story]

Moving now to another lab that tracks the trajectory of interstellar objects, they begin to make calculations and connect points on a graph. They note the location of key objects in the solar system as well as the other details that they're studying and, to their horror, they realize that this mystery object is indeed acting like a meteor. And it's headed straight toward Earth.

[conflict is introduced]

They continue to further detail the meteor and estimate its size based on the light-refraction patterns that they've recorded over the past several weeks. Finally, they estimate that the meteor is between six and ten kilometers wide and would make an impact greater than a thousand atomic blasts, enough to induce nuclear winter and possibly even nudge our planet out of its current orbit.

Again, the revelation does three incredibly important things: confirmation that the break in routine is significant, introduction of the problem of the story, and sets the forces of conflict into motion. Let's elaborate a little. While the problem of the story is introduced here, it's important to keep in mind that the characters have just noticed this problem. Why is this important? Because it's very likely that they will not understand the problem fully but rather will only have part of the picture. In our story above, later on, the research team will find out that rather than one large meteor, there are actually three medium-sized meteors headed towards Earth. For the introduction of conflict, I think it's always important to recognize that despite the refrain you hear constantly in popular culture, there are not "two sides to every story." There are usually about six. This is why I like to reiterate that the introduction of conflict introduces *at least* two parties (or perspectives) who are trying to solve the conflict in their favor. Why the convoluted language "in their favor"? I try to avoid the words "win" and "lose" because only in fairytales do things fall into such clear-cut categories. In addition, as soon as we move past a hero/villain story the terms make much less sense. A tsunami headed towards an island is not trying to "win" by killing everyone on the island; it's simply doing the thing that has been initiated by movement of undersea tectonic plates. It's doing what it does. Meanwhile, the islanders are scrambling to do what they need to do to evacuate. Rather than think of victory or defeat, it's far more useful to see the revelation as setting at least two "trains" into motion, each racing towards a point in the center, on track to collide with each other, each trying to get to the problem first and to solve it in their own favor.

A final point on conflict. In our story above, the family of conflict that this would fall into would be "Man vs. Nature." But there are many other categories of conflict too including "Man vs. Man," i.e. a classic hero/villain story. Others include "Man vs. Himself," "Man vs. Society," "Man vs. God," and the increasingly popular "Man vs. Technology." We can think of others as well. In our astronomy story above, the primary set of trains that are moving on a collision course are "Man vs. Nature," but since any complex story rarely involves only one level of conflict, we will also see "Man vs. Society" surface as the scientists try to get others to take them seriously, as well as "Man vs. Man" as countries vie to be the leaders in mounting a solution in order to take credit for saving humanity.

The Call

The next subsection of the action sequence is the call. The call is simply asking, "Who among us is going to rise up and do something about this problem?" It's important to keep in mind that the call, like the other subsections that we've come across and those that we'll come across soon, are not always as explicit as they might be in a fairytale. In a children's story, the queen, facing certain death due to an approaching dragon, might very explicitly tell her messengers to put a call out across the kingdom to find a hero among us. Or, perhaps most famously in *The Matrix* or the Academy awarding-winning film *Rocky*, the call will involve an actual ring of the telephone. But it's not always so blatant. Sometimes the call is distorted or even implied. For example,

47

consider Suzanne Collins' *The Hunger Games*. The games themselves are a forced selection of combatants. The call is present but it's not a voluntary call like other versions might be. Collins "fixes" this by having a kind of double call when Katniss offers to replace her sister. Or consider a story about a sister whose twin brother passes away. She's never lived without him and now has to find a way to move forward on terrifyingly shaky ground. She has not been called to deal with this problem. Fate has selected her. Again, an involuntary call is still a call.

The Refusal of the Call

The other side of the coin of the call is the refusal of the call. This is exactly what it sounds like. When someone is chosen or selected to be the one to fix the problem, their natural tendency is to hesitate. Often more than just hesitate, the appointed person pleads for reconsideration. Just like most of us in real life, characters in stories often feel inadequate and unable to solve important problems. We offer to assist but certainly not to lead the effort. We have too much else going on. We have impairments that make us less than ideal. We have no experience taking on a crisis like this. We have too much to lose. Moreover, we're not ready for the change that an embrace of the call would entail. Things might not be perfect now but they're predictable. Change is scary, even when it's potentially a change for the better.

As we noted with the call itself, the refusal too might be distorted or minimized. When one of two friends falls off of a canoe and into the river, the other friend jumps in even though she's terrified of water. There's no time for a cost/benefit analysis. When the house is on fire, the cat may not want to, but she's going to find her kitten, grab him, and dart out to find a way to get through the flames to safety. So the refusal can take on many forms. It can be a drawn out process of stubborness or begging for mercy. Or can be a fleeting moment of dread that a character has to immediately push past out of the necessity of the situation.

Regardless of how the refusal is overcome, it must be overcome or the story would end right there. The would-be hero always has the option to kill himself and prevent being thrown forward. Outside of an emergency situation that forces forward progression, how is the refusal overcome in a story? Usually one of three ways. The weakest of the forces is social pressure (though for many people this is the first to come to mind). This includes peer pressure, pressure from society, pressure from work, friends, family, and others. Just like in real life, these resonate at first as powerful sources of pressure, but they're really not. The person is weighing their fears and responsibilities on the one hand and what a few colleagues or cousins want them to do on the other. It's rarely enough to move someone towards accepting the call. The second force is torment from ephemeral sources. This might take the form of nightmares or visions that persistently eat away at our defenses, costing us sleep and weakening our resolve: the nagging, relentless feeling inside that not doing something about this problem will emotionally destroy us, making simply submitting to it the lesser of two evils. (As an interesting side note, the version of this force in ancient stories would usually be torment by God until the would-be hero finally acquiesces.)

And the final, most powerful force is personalization. The problem goes from being an abstract one to one that personaly involves an individual who now must accept the call that everyone, including himself, has been refusing to answer up until now. Imagine, tragically, that neighborhood children are disappearing one by one every few weeks as they play outside. No one knows what to do about these abductions. But it's finally when one particular mother faces the disappearance of her own child that she feels moved to act. This is personalization.

The Quest

The quest is by far the easiest subsection of all the action subsections to wrap your mind around. The refusal is overcome and the would-be hero embarks on the quest to solve the problem. In other words, she begins the mission of the story—again, usually to obtain something or to obtain freedom from something. There are two extremely important things to keep in mind at this point, however. First, the main character nearly always still holds all the doubts about herself that she had before. She's capable of acknowledging those but also recognizing the need (or want) to move forward towards what she assumes is likely failure to solve this intimidating problem. This is important. We need to remember that in nearly every story she's moving ahead with trepidation and hasn't been transformed simply by deciding to (or being forced to) accept the mission. She may even be going forward with a kind of cynical pride that her failure will show others that she was right about being a poor choice as appointed problem-solver back at the refusal.

The other important thing to keep in mind is that, as we mentioned earlier, the true nature of the problem is fuzzy at this point. Our scientists at first faced one meteor only to find out later that it was actually three. A hero is embarking on the quest to solve the problem with only the initial understanding of the problem at hand. She will very rarely be fully correct about this. A great metaphor to think of is from *Super Mario Brothers*, the classic Nintendo video game. Mario is searching for Princess Peach, who has been kidnapped. From Mario's perspective he's heard that if he goes ahead a little, climbs through some trees, swims past some fish, and jumps on a few enemies, that he'll then make it to a castle where the princess will be and he'll save the day. He does all of that, and when he finally makes it past the spiked-turtle guarding the tunnel at the end of the castle, he finds Toad, long-time protector of the Mushroom Kingdom, who breaks the news to him that he's done well but the princess is actually in a different castle. Embarking on the quest, Mario does not know that. No hero does. From the perspective of many would-be heroes, although they are reluctantly embarking, the saving grace (they think) is at least the mission will be short. Not quite.

Complications

The complications subsection refers to the fact that the mission is not as easy to accomplish as the main character thinks it will be.

Not only do unforeseen circumstances arise, but, just like Mario, his initial understanding of the problem starts to change: it becomes more complicated to solve than he first thinks. For every step of progress forward, the end goal seems that much further away. Very often side missions come to the forefront. So making what seems like a straight-forward journey from A to B, suddenly involves a whole bunch of mini-steps between them. These side missions take the short arrow from start to finish that was on her map and push it off in all kinds of directions and loops as it meanders towards the destination. This is why the complications stage most often ends up being the vast majority of the actual story.

Sometimes in the story design work that I do I'm asked to comment on something that involves separating story from character. For example, I might get a question like these: "What do you think about character X put in a story like Y?" or "What's more important, character or plot?" The truth is that these kinds of questions make no sense because character and story are not two things that you can pull apart. There are threads that connect them and that make them part of the same fabric. If you can pull them apart, then there's usually something very wrong with the story. We can see exactly why that's the case when we look closer here at the complications stage.

Think about the complications stage in the context of what's come before it. The character has reluctantly accepted the quest either through personalization, coercion, overzealous bravado, or some other means. He's either already getting a sense (or is about to get a sense) that the problem isn't exactly what he thought it was at first. He's a mix of curiosity and nerves. He's understandably afraid of the unknown. What the obstacles, or the trials as Campbell would call them, do is to give the hero a chance to not only learn more about the problem but more about himself too. The obstacles are forcing him to dig down into his character to find an inner resolve that may be under the surface, hidden in plain view. He's learning more about his fears, talents, ambition, courage, virtue, and worldview. In fact, these are coming into focus, perhaps even some of them for the first time. They not only come into focus, but they change depending on what the obstacle in front has in store for him. This is called character development. And it *is* the story. There's no other story that's the real story that this character is tied up in. The story is the interplay between the events, crises, and breakthroughs that happen and how the character responds to and grows as a result of those events.

If we step back a little and look at the complications stage we can make an important realization. Very often we fixate on the hero getting closer to her goal. This makes sense. After all, once the problem is introduced the anxiety automatically arises as to whether a solution will be found. For a story designer, counter-intuitively, it's the shadow that's more important than the hero's progress towards the sun. In other words, it's failure, not success that is of supreme importance. Failure is the fuel that pushes the entire story forward. Failure to obtain her goal until she completes side missions reveals the true nature of the problem. Failure to succeed right away forces her to start to search through her talents and perception of herself. And failure to obtain her goal starts to eliminate her choices for how to ultimately resolve this problem one by one, cutting off the paths of least resistance until only the more challenging solution avenues are left. Yes, the story receiver is usually preoccupied with whether, how, and if the hero is moving towards her goal, but as a story designer you should be far more focused on why she's failing to move forward and what opportunities that creates in the story's development. These setbacks force her to search for what she's made of and to find courage and abilities that she didn't even know were there, thereby growing and becoming a stronger, more capable version of herself. Adapting the words of the Irish playwriting giant Samuel Beckett in *Worstward Ho!*, a story's hero looks to "Try again. Fail again. Fail better." This is the cycle that replays itself over and over again as the story proceeds.

There are two important things to mention about the obstacles. First, they should be getting larger as the story moves forward. This is not only true because we've come to expect it in any story we watch, read, or listen to. It also makes logical sense. To solve any problem, we always opt for the easiest solution, the aforementioned path of least resistance and minimal risk. If that doesn't work out, we move to the next easiest solution, and so on. As this pattern continues, future solution attempts are more involved, more complicated, and more challenging to carry out. The same dynamic is at play in a story. Our hero tries this, and when it doesn't work she tries that, then that, then something new, and so on moving from the obvious angles to the more complicated angles. Moreover, even when she does appear to find a solution, she quickly realizes that that solution only corresponds to an incomplete version of the problem's true nature and so she must now keep trying. So, like an avalanche, the problem may in fact be, or appear to be, small, only to get larger and larger over time, triggering a solution strategy reevaluation.

The second thing to keep in mind as a story designer is that the minimum number of obstacles in a story is three. Note that I'm saying minimum, not maximum. In many stories, like for example the *Harry Potter* series, the obstacles number perhaps into the hundreds. When I ask my students why they think this is, sometimes they suggest that three might be necessary because the character needs time to develop. I like the answer, but it's the tail wagging the dog. The character developing is the *result* of the obstacles not the reason for them in the first place. Few texts that I've read even speculate about why this minimum number is three, most of them opting simply to state it and to move on. But I will venture to provide a reason based on my observations. There are three core things that the obstacles do and so if there are only three of them then each plays a certain role. The first obstacle serves to focus the hero. The hero is stepping out of his familiar world and into the world of the unknown as he embarks on this adventure. The first obstacle gives him a clue about how this new world works, what its rules are, what its weaknesses are, and how its strengths are manifested. In a sense, it's there to introduce him to the new battleground. The second obstacle serves to somewhat (or fully) clarify the nature of the problem. As we've been discussing, the hero thinks the problem is one thing only to find out that it's more complicated than it seems. The second obstacle does that and increases the tension because of what it reveals. The third obstacle is crucial because it sets up the crescendo of the action sequence as we will see in the next two subsections. It gives rise to a moment that will be the centerpiece of the story's primary change. None of this is possible without an imposing third and final obstacle that looms over the other two. I believe that's why the minimum number is three.

In closing this section, I want to return to a critical point that I made earlier about this being the universal story structure for both fiction and nonfiction stories. You might be saying to yourself that, sure, if you're a game designer or a fiction writer then this makes sense, but real life doesn't always fall into such nice patterns. *But it does.* Think about it this way. If you're telling a nonfiction, true life story at a cocktail party and you explain every moment that happened in your story—every single moment—it could go on for hours, days, months, even years if you got into enough detail about every nuance. Meanwhile, the party ended six months ago. But of course you don't do that. You only tell *parts* of the story (or what you might have called the *important parts* before reading this book). Well, what *are* the important parts? These parts that I've just explained and the ones that I'm about to explain are the important parts. This is the arrangement that yields the best story that those combined events can make. This is the arrangement that yields a memorable story.

Catastrophe

Let's recap our hero's journey so far. There was a break in her world's normal routine, a break that proved significant. This break in routine pointed out a problem that someone needed to solve and also brought to light some ways of possibly solving it. The constituents or "the people" that the would-be hero is a member of made a call out for someone to step up. Our hero, through duty or force, stepped forward. She mounted a solution gameplan only to find out that things weren't going to be quite as straight-forward as she thought. One thing that surprised her is that she went into this thinking that she was a very poor choice to be the one to do something about this, but, little by little, she's reevaluating that. You could even say that the way that she feels about her own capability and potential is changing. As she pushed past the blocks in her path one after the next, she's feeling better and better. Her confidence is rising. That's where we are now. And that's where things are about to fall apart.

I like to think about the catastrophe this way. Think of our hero's path as a line or arrow, pointed towards the ultimate problem which must be confronted then solved. Now think of the obstacles that have come so far as circles along the path of that arrow that are getting bigger and bigger and bigger as the story goes on. And so here we are at what might very well be the final circle, the final obstacle. And as the fog clears it comes into sight on the horizon. Only it's not a circle. It's a massive square. And it's five times bigger than the circle that came before it. How does our main character feel? The same way that you would. She's crushed. Destroyed. Gutted. It's not that she feels stuck. She feels utterly defeated because for all intents and purposes she *is* defeated. Part of the transformation that's been happening within her has taught her about herself, about the latent abilities and talents that she didn't even know she had. But it's all apparently for naught. The very nature of this last obstacle is totally unlike the previous ones. It's not just a larger and scarier version of the ones before it. It's fundamentally different. All that growth and all those recent insights look to be useless after all.

The first thing she does when she realizes this is to retreat from the "battlefield." This means physically removing herself from the place where she's had to confront the previous obstacles. If the story's about a lawyer who has been in court or in her office up all night finding ways to cross-examine key witnesses, and the next morning everything blows up in her face, now she goes back to her apartment, or even better, her summer cabin to sulk and to lament how progress is no longer possible. A side effect of this retreat from the battlefield is that her normal ways of thinking about the problems she's faced are also pushed to the side. She's no longer locked in like she once was when she was on edge as obstacle after obstacle was coming her way. Her mind is free, in a sense, to roam wherever it wants to roam. This break from the action, unbeknownst to her, is exactly what she needs. And it creates the tiniest, indirect crack in the shell of the towering square in front of her.

One of the things she can't help but think about in this recess is the way she approached solving this problem. She tried this and that and so many things, and, despite the progress, wasn't able to complete the task. In going through these strategies she starts to wonder if in fact she *did* go down every possible path. Notice what's happening. Instead of looking forward at the obstacle, she's starting to look at herself more and more. Getting away from where the obstacles were has been just the thing that she needed. As she continues to do this, she comes to a realization, a realization that leads to the next section, and the final subsection of the action sequence.

The Critical Choice

One caveat as we enter this final section of the action sequence. I recognize that the below dissection of the critical choice may be a lot to digest for the non-storyteller. I considered finding a happy midway point by simply calling it an important choice that the hero has to make that puts everything on the line and gives the mission one last try, but that did not feel adequate to me. Since this book has sought to be thorough in explaining each of the other subsections, I will do the same for this section in spite of its nuances and complexity. In the end, the critical choice is about looking within to find the courage to move forward regardless of the odds against emerging successful. That's it in a nutshell. But if you're curious about the details, keep reading.

The realization that the hero makes is that rather than fixate on the weaknesses of the obstacle in front of her, she must focus on her own weaknesses. Maybe in fact there's something holding her back from finding the courage to confront this final obstacle. In my class on secondary character archetypes I call this thing holding her back the "needy ghost." There is something from her past, something that is cataloged as trauma or pain or fear that has been holding her back from being the best version of herself. This needy ghost has been haunting her for a long time. In fact, back in the exposition section I mentioned that the "what" of who, what, where, and when, is more complicated than it may seem. This is why. The what was what does the character want the most? Remember, this is *before* the problem of the story is introduced. So what is it that the character wants, or, more accurately, *needs*, before all this? *To placate the needy ghost.* To face the past. To stand up to what's holding her back. To confront her fear. To deal with the long-standing problem that came before the story mission.

So the critical choice is the choice that she makes once she makes these realizations. She realizes that she *can* in fact attempt to overcome the final obstacle by realizing that the true obstacle is within herself. In fact, it's very likely that this final external obstacle reminds her in some indirect way of that internal obstacle that she's facing. In other words, the outer turmoil reflects the inner turmoil. She connects the dots and finds a way to push forward. I will talk more about this later, but a side-effect of her finding the strength to push forward in this moment instigates a deep connection that's possible right here on the part of the story receiver. The fears and trauma that characters have often echo our own, and the stories that we cherish most in our lives most likely say something about what we've had to (or might long to) confront ourselves. As we can see with the critical choice, the more we unpack this moment, the more important it gets.

But what does the critical choice actually look like? The critical choice is essentially an extremely difficult choice for the hero to make. It's something that she does not want to do but now believes that it marks the only way forward. So this added existential crisis makes the challenge even more extreme than it already is. She's fighting the inner demon as well as the outer demon. The critical choice usually involves some form of risk. So the stakes, or the consequences of failure suddenly shoot up. Failing the story mission is not the only thing at risk anymore. What else is at risk? Her reputation. Her standing in the community. Her ability to pursue her dreams. Her sanity. Her own personal safety. Or perhaps the most high-stakes of all, the lives of those she cares about most in the world. All of these are very likely ingredients in the critical choice.

Earlier I suggested that because of how important it is, the revelation is probably the second most important part of the universal story structure. The critical choice is the single most important part because of the way it brings the story full circle, reminding us (to paraphrase William Faulkner) that the past is not dead. It's not even past. In other words, to move forward, our hero must first look back.

These are the eight subsections of the action sequence, by far the most complicated section of the universal story structure. So much is happening here that alternative story models slice this section up into additional broader strokes with names like "hook," "point of no return," and "rising action." I don't find these quite so useful, especially the last of these, since from the very get-go of the first obstacle the action and tension are rising. I find it far more useful to look at the eight dimensions of the subsections I've detailed here. I mentioned the gears of a watch earlier. Remove a part of the mainspring, escapement, or wheel train and you create a problem somewhere down the line, a problem that can't be ignored or brushed off. This is what non-memorable storytelling does. Writing that pays little or no attention to this structure for commercial purposes, for unrealistic fear of low attention spans, or out of simple ignorance of how powerful stories are put together, will entail all kinds of strange choices about what to include or what not to include. Entire sections will be skipped, character development will be an aside, and the stakes will always remain low or irrelevant to the audience or reader.

There is so much misunderstanding about these topics that you see endless debates online or in print about why some stories just don't "work" or why the plots of certain stories just don't "come together." And the flipside too—an inability to suggest what exactly makes a story "great," "classic," or "unforgettable." The answer lies in the story designer's understanding of the relationship and connections between these elements and his willingness to take the time needed to find them.

ACTION

The action sequence is the vast majority of the story and is broken down into several subsections.

The break in routine, or inciting incident, is when something unusual or unexpected happens. The revelation as to why this break in routine is so important comes next.

The call refers to the solicitation or request for help that the group affected by the revelation makes. Who will take on the responsibility of fixing this situation?

The quest begins but immediately appears to be more complicated than initially thought. This is exacerbated by the fact that the full nature of the problem is slowly being revealed.

The obstacles increase in size and complexity as the main character inches towards confronting and attempting to solve the problem, only to face a moment of loss of hope called the catastrophe.

The main character's despair at the catastrophe is a hidden blessing because he realizes that there may indeed be a way forward, but it will involve a huge risk. It will mean making a critical choice.

Climax

The third major section of the story arc is the climax. The climax is incredibly simple to understand, but it's also incredibly important.

The climax is the moment that those two trains set into motion at the revelation finally collide. They've been slowly heading towards each other this entire time. And now, the tension is as high as it can be as these two forces confront each other, each trying to solve the problem in their own favor. It's the cop's big showdown with the jewel thief, the instant the tornado hits the village, or the moment of the doctor's final attempt to inject what she thinks is the correct antidote formula into the suffering patient. (As an interesting sidenote, remember back in the revelation I mentioned that at least two trains are set into motion? As we added, in real life, there are rarely just two sides to any story or two forces trying to win. When the biggest train hits our hero, that's the climax. When other trains hit our hero those are the preceding obstacles including the one that creates the catastrophe.)

The climax is obviously incredibly important, so much so that it has its own section. However, when looking at the interconnections between all of the elements, I actually think it's slightly more useful to consider the climax to be an extension of the critical choice since they always go together. It's like the two moments are shaped like a dumbell. Yes, they do have their own characteristics, but one simply yields its shape to become the other one. They are not fully separated entities. The central reason for this is that the climax also represents the primary moment of change in the story. Remember earlier that we talked about the Big Three: change in circumstance, change in insight, or change in relationship. Those may have been slowly in flux as the action section continued but here at the climax is where they change the most. But if you think about this for a second, where does the big change actually *start* to ramp up? You could very well argue in many stories that the major change starts at the critical choice and then crystallizes at the climax. The change moment is more than just the pinpoint of the climax moment. It covers a slightly wider timeframe, a timeframe that encompasses the critical choice too. This is why the two moments are, I think, really part of the same longer moment. In the end, it doesn't quite matter how you look at the climax on a technical level. It's still extremely important. This detail only comes into play later if and when you experiment with story order.

There is a major fear on the part of many story designers that their climax will fall flat. If the stakes are high, the character has developed, and deep-seated anxieties that are reflected in the obstacles are confronted, then it won't fall flat. But nevertheless, the understandable worry exists. So what many designers will do is to create what's called a "topsy-turvy" moment. What happens here is that at the moment the trains collide we don't see clearly what's happened. There is a collision and a fog in the resulting chaos, a question mark about which side the coinflip is landing on. The purpose of this is to elongate the climax, to build the tension even more, and to reduce the possibility that it goes by too quickly and thus fails to make the impact intended.

CLIMAX

The climax is where the two conflict "trains" finally collide.

To avoid the climax going by too quickly, the story will often include a moment of ambiguity.

At the climax, the "trains" represent the forces of conflict. Traditionally, forms of conflict include the following and more:

"Man vs. Man"   "Man vs. Self"
"Man vs. Nature"   "Man vs. Society"
"Man vs. God"   "Man vs. Technology"

Resolution

The fourth section of the universal story structure is the resolution. Simply put, it's the aftermath of the climax. But there are several important details to mention.

The aftermath of the climax is obviously supremely important in a story. The audience or the reader finds out who won or lost. Did the jewel thief outsmart the cop? Did the villagers find shelter from the tornado? Did the last-ditch version of the formula of the vaccine finally work? In understanding the broad strokes of story structure I used the words win and lose, but I rarely use them in analyzing the finer details. In stories for adults, whether it's a short story, a novel, a memoir, or The Base, it's rarely ever a simple matter of winning or losing. If you succeed in solving the story problem but have to betray your best friend to do it, is that a win or a loss? If the disease's cure works but is so expensive that it's only available to the super rich, is that a win or a loss? If the victim of a crime sues the perpetrator and gets a massive financial settlement but has to spend the rest of his life in a hospital bed, is that a win or a loss? It's obviously a mix of both. So the resolution is the aftermath of the climax in all of its black, white, and grey shades.

The resolution also now alters something that was established in the exposition. At the end of the exposition I noted that part of its role is to establish the routine, normal world for the characters. Pushing ahead now to the resolution, the normal world from the exposition is suddenly the "old normal." The resolution establishes the new normal, the normal that has been created as a result of the change at the climax. It's impossible to say how much of the new world is "required" to introduce. Story designers may show the ripple effects of the change throughout the new normal world or simply just hint at it. There is no one way to create this. What's critical though is that the new normal is marked or created in the first place.

Resolutions are incredibly hard to do well. The reason is probably self-evident to you. Your audience has been building up expectations throughout the whole story. They very likely have silently ventured guesses about what's going to happen. Throw into the mix the combination of victory and defeat that will, hopefully strike the bittersweet chord that author William Goldman implied when he said that a resolution should "give the audience what they want but not what they expect." Serve the audience a dessert that they're craving but take a risk by bringing to the table something other than what they ordered.

This is in fact so challenging that some story designers opt out of the resolution. Very often when I'm working with new writers I will see this. The story will end at the climax. I will ask them why. And they will tell me that this is just how they write. The problem is that even the most skilled writers have a very difficult time pulling this off in a way that satisfies readers. You could argue that an unspoken promise that a story designer has made by telling the story in the first place is that we're going to at least get a glimpse of what happened to the main characters. The more details in the story the more emotional investment on the part of the reader or audience. When they're deprived of this, the backlash can be tremendous and feel like a betrayal. This negative reaction is a very common price to pay for what's called the open resolution. An open resolution means the lack of a resolution. Can some storytellers find commercial success with open resolutions? Yes. It's happened. But it's rare.

Sometimes, if you look closely you will see that some parts of the resolution are open and some are closed, mitigating the potential negative impact of the fully open resolution. The flipside of the open resolution is the closed resolution, which means having a resolution, which the vast majority of stories do. Yes, it is not easy by any means. But I strongly recommend climbing the mountain rather than giving up beforehand. Just like every other story element, the more you practice the better you'll be at it. Creating stories with open resolutions is not a habit I would recommend until the closed resolution is attempted.

RESOLUTION

NEW Establishes the new world
(or the new normal) as a result
of the change in the climax

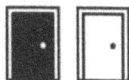

Can be open or closed, with
closed meaning having a
resolution and open meaning
stopping at the climax

While all quality storytelling is challenging,
the resolution is one of the most difficult
parts of a story to build because there's
nearly always a mix of winning and losing.
It's important to be honest about what that
mix is.

Denouement

The fifth and final element of the universal story structure is the denouement. Two important notes. First is that, as I mentioned above when we discussed terms like "rising action" before the climax, there are many different story models and terms for story structure elements. For many models, everything that happens after the climax is considered the denouement. No problem. We can just recognize that as another version of what I'm calling the resolution. I happen to think that two distinct things can happen after the climax so I've separated them into two categories: resolution then denouement. The second point is that you might remember at the outset that I stated there were 4.5 elements of the universal story structure. Why the half section? Because unlike the others, the denouement is not required. Sometimes it's present and sometimes it isn't. The word "universal" means that it must be present, but since this is not universal then it can't be treated the same as the other elements. If I were to write out the five parts of the universal story structure, I would write this one out in parentheses.

What I'm calling the denouement is when the story is over but there are additional added details about what happens later. The name for this in writing is of course an epilogue. We see this in visual storytelling too. After the final fade out of a documentary film text will very often come on the screen and tell us what happened to the characters in the months or years after the events depicted. The key trait of the denouement is that it always moves forward in time. Earlier we had the idea that exposition is what happens before the story starts. Well, the denouement is what happens after the story ends. The story is over and additional information is added. This can add a lot, especially in nonfiction stories, but there's no way it could be considered "mandatory." Again, the key detail here is that the denouement always moves forward in time. If it moves backwards in time then it's a part of the exposition or backstory.

DENOUEMENT

When the story is over but more details are added

The denouement always moves forward in time, never backward

Just like the exposition is what happens before the story starts, the denouement is what happens after the story ends. Just like other elements, the denouement can actually come earlier than the very end of the story.

The 4.5 Elements

After going through this chapter, I'm sure you can tell (if you couldn't before) why I balk at the overuse of the word story. There are even best-selling titles propped up on display shelves at your local bookstore right now, extolling the virtues of five-word "stories" because they elicit strong reactions. Sure, words, since they're all metaphors after all, are connected with ideas and emotion just like the image of a fireside coffee is, or a swastika is, but they're not stories. It not only doesn't get us anywhere to imply they are, but it's actually counter-productive to anyone seriously looking to use storytelling systematically and effectively. Let's let provocative images be what they are and not insist on using some bizarre literary alchemy to make them into something they're not. Let's instead look with our own eyes at the undeniable patterns that exist in storytelling.

These are the 4.5 elements of the universal story structure: exposition, action, climax, resolution, and denouement. If a story is information that has been packaged in a particular way to make it unforgettable, then this is the package. This is the arrangement. This is not a formula. It's important to reiterate that because it can feel like one to readers new to this concept. A formula is like a recipe. Add this amount of this ingredient, mix it with this exact amount of that ingredient, sprinkle them both with this ingredient, and you've got your dish. But when you go to cooking school you don't learn how to make four specific dishes. You learn how to make *any* dish. You learn the underlying principles of flavor combinations and cooking techniques that make any meal come together. To return to the bridge metaphor.

The universal story structure is not a plan for how to make a specific bridge. It's the underlying set of principles that allow you to make any bridge you want. When it comes to structural integrity we can debate what the bridge's materials, width, or color should be, but we can't debate the physical requirements needed to prevent it from collapsing. Rather than confining, I believe that the universal story structure is actually freeing because there are infinite combinations for how you can put a story together and still make one that stands. It unlocks your ability to push your storytelling to its limits and not to have to worry about where structural flaws might surface. It gives you a box to play in, and in that box you can do anything you want.

It is extremely important to reiterate the flexibility of the elements' order. In this chapter I had to present the element of the story arc in some fashion, so I opted for the one that would dovetail it with a fairytale in order to help us understand some of those initial subsections of the action sequence. But remember, as long as the pieces are there, the order can essentially be whatever the story designer wants it to be. Perhaps the most extreme mainstream example of this is the film *Memento*, that's told entirely backwards in time. The causality and exposition come to the viewer in reverse but the film is totally comprehensible nevertheless.

I do want to put forth two points of caution, however, before we accept the idea that a story can be sliced up at random and reassembled without any cost. I believe that the full picture of the new normal established in the resolution, if presented early in a story, loses its most forceful impact if the audience has not been introduced to any aspect of the exposition (the old normal). This is one of the costs of pure randomization. The second point is that the critical choice/climax "dumbbell" moment is the culmination of the tension building in the action sequence. It's meaning is derived not only from the failures that have come before it but from the deep-seated trauma, anxiety, or fear (the needy ghosts discussed earlier) that are about to be confronted. Therefore, putting the climax first is like trying to play the final beat of an orchestra drum crescendo without the crescendo part. It just becomes a beat with only a shadow of significance when in fact this moment is the most consequential in the entire story. Pure randomization is possible but I believe these two caveats, or exceptions, are worth noting.

In looking at these universal story structure elements, we've been operating at a certain scale. In other words, we've seen pieces from a distance that allows us to notice how they operate and how they fit with other parts of the story structure. That level of approximation is very useful because from that vantage point we can see that each part is indispensable because it contributes a necessary ingredient to the story as a whole. But before closing this chapter, there are two places that I would like to zoom in a little deeper on in order to discuss some subtleties about this structure that are more qualitative than quantitative: two characteristics of a memorable story that go beyond the mechanics of the arrangement.

First, there's one important dimension of the critical choice that's gone unmentioned so far. I mentioned before that the catastrophe sets the stage for the hero to begin a process of mental searching. Even if he doesn't realize it consciously, he's analyzing the nature of the final obstacle, what's come before it, if there is a light at the end of the tunnel, and/or whether the journey's come to an end. He may very well often do something else that's important in this contemplation stage. He may start to question his deepest assumptions about the world itself. I added the terms virtue, worldview, and ambition into the mix when I talked about the types of attributes that surface and develop in a character during the action sequence. But what does it really mean for those to develop? I mean that previous conclusions about them may be reconsidered. So our hero might have a strong sense of what he believes is right or wrong. Suddenly, in the lead up to the critical choice, he's going over these beliefs and asking himself how sound his conclusions really are. He may have a strong stance that serving society's best interest requires him to do what the majority asks of him. And yet he might now wonder whether leadership means taking an unpopular stance from time to time. He may have a belief that his moral compass gives him a very reliable indication of who is good and who is evil. Suddenly, he might entertain the idea that there is a good and evil inside of all of us that can be nurtured by different situations and influences. So the critical choice is also a place where these fundamental core interpretations of the world can be interrogated by the main character. This is crucial because it very well might be the case that one of these reinterpretations is a key ingredient in the cocktail of insights that allows the critical choice to happen. Indeed, very often the

77

centerpiece of a main character's breakthrough in a story involves confronting and correcting a long-standing misinterpretation about their reality.

The second next-level detail that's worth mentioning concerns relatability. Relatability refers to getting your listeners to connect with your story in a way that's relevant to their own lives. It's not so much about asking them to put themselves in your character's shoes (although it could mean that as well), but it's more about finding ways to connect the key turning points and struggles in your story with parallel turning points and struggles in their lives. All of this falls under the umbrella of nurturing universality in your story. In a nutshell, universality centers on finding universal themes that arise for everyone so that no matter what the specific details of a story might be, it will find a way to touch any person's heart or mind. This is obvious when we look at science fiction or fantasy. The everyday details of the worlds that the storyteller has created are things that the reader cannot physically relate to in any way. So how does the story designer keep the audience engaged and elicit emotional reactions in such a foreign context?

Through universal themes. In my work I break down universal themes into three "tiers," meaning themes that are simply powerful verses themes strong enough to carry an entire story from start to finish. Some of the big ones are injustice, duty, empathy, forgiveness, and greed, but the biggest are loyalty, betrayal, freedom, power, redemption, survival, and, of course, love. So when you hear about relatability in a story it comes down to these themes that are woven throughout. These themes, and the characters' takes on these themes, are very often showcased the most at the critical choice.

This is The Base

The universal story structure detailed above is simultaneously the structure of the story I'm calling The Base in this book. The Base is a story about a person, a hero for the purposes of our structure. In a business setting this will very likely be you although it could be someone else. The structure can be scaled up or down as needed. As long as the pieces are there, size and scope are not important. Perhaps most crucially, once you've mastered The Base, it's a small step towards mastering the other seven stories for businesses and professionals because of how much those other stories rely on The Base. In fact, The Base can take the form of an oral story delivered in front of a group of people, but it's also the way to build towards a book, short story, screenplay, or something larger.

Perhaps you read this chapter over the course of several days, or perhaps you read it all in one go. However you went through this, right now, this very moment, is an important moment. It's very likely that for many of you this is the first time that you're learning about these elements and their specific story roles and characteristics. I have no doubt that either consciously or subconsciously story ideas have been coming into your mind. The brain is an incredible organ that's working tremendously hard analyzing, processing, and cataloging vast amounts of past and present stimuli even when we're focusing on something else. This is an opportunity for you to see what's there, a chance to see what stories you have and how they can be brought to life by this structure. Keep reading. The next chapter will introduce the next seven stories and more. But before that, take a moment to catch your breath and to let your mind wander. Let go for a second and see what comes up. Write it down and add one brick at a time. You may be surprised at what you can build when these ideas are merging for you all at the same time.

CHAPTER 3 – THE 8 STORIES

The Heart of It

It's time to transition to the heart of this book. The eight stories for business and professionals are the adjustments that are made to The Base to correspond to the needs of the moment. We're not talking about the eight stories as in "The Tortoise and the Hare" or "The Prodigal Son" but rather about story styles. In fact, we're not talking about *any* fictional stories anymore at all since all eight stories will be nonfiction. The subject matter of the stories is something that we'll tackle in the final chapter. But why is concentrating on story formats so important? Because the effectiveness of any story is a combination of what you say and how you say it, and story formatting provides a guide towards striking this balance.

This book could have been just an expanded version of The Base, simply looking at what a story is and some of the factors that go into building a great one. But in the course of my research when I noticed these eight distinct patterns, it made a lot more sense to take the advice to the next level. After all, there are plenty of strong texts on the art of storytelling. Instead, I wanted to create a resource that was compact enough to be inviting and clear enough so that you could find your needed format quickly and start building and modifying right away.

For story analysts, one of the most exciting developments over the past ten-plus years has been seeing how much storytelling is being recognized as the most important tool in business communication. The key word is "sticky." How can you make your message stick in the minds of team members, shareholders, and customers? Use storytelling. And I agree of course. But I also believe that sometimes different situations call for adjustments. To keep cricket captivating for younger fans, the 20/20 format was developed by Stuart Robinson of the England and Wales Cricket Board in the 1990s. Likewise, stories too may have to be resized based on the needs of the moment. This chapter explores each size along with the priorities and considerations that arise with those size adjustments. I will also include some situations where each particular story format is useful. These are of course only partial recommendations. You're likely to think of far more scenarios where some of the stories about to be discussed would be effective. I'll conclude each format with a pro tip that will make a dramatic difference in the quality of your storytelling regardless of format. I believe that organizing my ideas the way I've done here creates an extremely useful tool for you. Building a personal story about a major crossroads in your life? Turn to The Base and The Maker. Developing a 30-second pitch? Turn to The Capsule. Invited to share your work and ideas in front of a large audience? Turn to The Talk. So this book is in fact a catalog of powerful storytelling attributes, but it's also a guide that helps you pinpoint and prioritize exactly what you need in a given situation.

To some extent, we already know that different situations call for different considerations in storytelling. Everyone has heard the refrain "know your audience." Yes, it's absolutely true that the audience is a major factor in how you design your story. But to consider that the chief factor that alters the story approach is incomplete. It's certainly important, and I will discuss more about this below, but the situational picture is much larger and the influencing factors on a story's focus are much more diverse than a singular focus on the audience implies. Moreover, in public events you don't always know your audience. So if audience make-up is your principle design guide, you're in the dark when that remains a question mark.

One note before starting. I've included a brief summary of The Base here in this chapter simply as a reminder. If you've made your way to this section of the book without reading the previous chapter, I can't stress how much I recommend going back to read the previous section. It's like we're learning how to make cakes. These story formats are like explaining wedding, sheet, birthday, cheese, and cup cakes. In other words, the way you can slice up and reshape the cake. The Base shows you how to make the actual cake part. Without understanding The Base, there's a severe limit on how useful the descriptions of each of the story formats that follow will be.

Story #1 The Base

As outlined in detail in the previous chapter, The Base comprises exposition, action, climax, and resolution. It may or may not also have a denouement. The exposition is the foundation: the who, what, where, and when of the story. This orients the reader and invites them into the story world. The exposition also establishes the normal, routine world for the main character. The action sequence has many subsections and starts with the break in routine. Briefly put, when this routine is broken, the problem of the story is introduced along with the forces of conflict looking to solve the problem in their own favor. In a call and refusal of the call, a request is put out for someone to come forward and lead the effort to solve this problem. Through one means or another, the refusal is overcome and the quest begins.

Unforeseen obstacles present themselves during this mission, and in overcoming these obstacles one by one the main character learns about the world, the true nature of the problem at hand, and about himself. There will come a point when he just cannot go on, which is called the catastrophe. At this moment he's forced to reflect on his progress. In this reflection period he realizes that he must make a critical choice if he wants to move forward. Embarking on this risky choice that he wishes he didn't have to make, he's able to give the mission one final shot. When he does that, he's able to be present for the collision of the parties that were trying to solve the problem in their favor (of which he is one). This is the climax. The climax causes a significant change. This change results in a new external world, internal world, or important relationship development for the character (and sometimes all three). This new normal is the resolution. The structure concludes with the denouement, the only optional element in The Base which pushes forward in time to explain what happened to the characters or situation after the story finished.

The Base is not only indispensable for a wide range of story situations, but it also generates the source material from which to build any story format of any shape and size. The Base is collecting the clay. Once you collect the clay you can shape it any way you see fit or opt to use portions of it to create compact or specialized forms of sculptures or vessels.

Situations where The Base is useful include essentially every storytelling scenario:

- Introducing yourself to a group of people
- Performing at a live storytelling event
- Developing or enlarging case studies
- Writing about a key moment in your life for a short, personal, true story
- Writing nonfiction as part of a memoir, biography, or other book
- Writing fiction as part of a novel, novella, or short story

- Writing film and video scripts, screenplays, or audio stories
- Creating source material out of which any of the other seven story formats can be formed

The
BASE

The Universal Story Structure

EXPOSITION

The foundation of the "house" including the who, what, where, and when that create the normal, routine world

ACTION

The break in routine, realization of the problem, start of conflict, call to action, obstacles, failure, and final choice

CLIMAX

The point of highest tension where the forces of conflict finally meet, where the most change happens

RESOLUTION

As a result of the change that happened in the climax, a new normal is established: the resolution

DENOUEMENT

When the story is over, if there is more story about what happened moving forward, this is the denouement

Story #2 The Maker

This story is called The Maker because it refers to the story that made you who you are. So when we look at The Base, we can imagine using that structure for all kinds of stories: strange ones, funny ones, dramatic ones, instructional ones, and even scary ones. And when we look at the bullet-pointed potential uses for The Base above we can see just how foundational it is. The Base can be used as the set of building blocks of any story across genres, formats, lengths, and mediums. If The Base emcompasses all story possiblilties, then The Maker is just one specific slice of that.

The Maker refers to a true, personal story that centers on a major turning point in your life. The Maker is always told from the first-person point of view, meaning through your eyes. So it's something that happened to you, told by you, that uses The Base as the general format but with some specific priorities. What's a major turning point? A major turning point is one where your life literally or figuratively could have gone in one direction or another, where this thing that happened was so consequential that you tend to think of your life in some sense as being divided into before this happened and after. It could involve a dramatic change in fortune (for the better or the worse) or a profound wake-up call when a cherished belief of yours turned out to be mistaken. It could center on someone you met, a project you did, a chance encounter, or the moment when you felt more alive than at any moment before. Whatever the event, it would break the surface at the inciting incident and a hint of just how consequential this was would be woven into the revelation.

A turning point is something with a lasting impact. In some sense, every day that follows after a major turning point is somehow colored by what happened in that moment. Whether it's a career choice, a personal commitment, or a new way of looking at the world, your eyes have been opened to something and it changed you at your core, compelling you to make certain choices and to not make others. I would argue that every adult has had at least one of these experiences if not more. I can personally think of four or five for me, where a switch went off in a moment of trauma or elation that shaped my personality forever. This is what The Maker captures. You share The Maker because you want your audience to know who you truly are. You want them to cut through the notoriously unreliable outward impression and to see what makes you tick deep down inside. You want to show them how this moment changed you, forged you.

In addition to being a personal, nonfiction story that follows The Base format closely, there's one other structural necessity for The Maker. The resolution, the denouement, or both must focus on exactly why this was a moment that shaped your life to such a major extent. It's crucial not to expect The Maker to speak for itself. So the resolution can detail the new normal and how these events gave birth to a new version of you or the denouement could begin with something along the lines of "Looking back, the reason that this had such a profound effect on me was because of X, Y, and Z." Or you could accomplish this task with a combination of both. This is different than The Base. In The Base, best practice is not to connect the dots, to never "step out" of the story, so to speak, but rather to let the audience or the reader come to their own conclusion about what the story is all about. So The Maker is more explicit in that way. In the Maker, you tell the audience how your personality was fundamentally formed in some way by this thing that happened. (Following each story's pro tip, I have included a graphic that summarizes the key concepts at the heart of each story format.)

Some situations where The Maker is useful:

- Speaking to a group of people about what drives you
- Presenting in a highly personal setting about what inspires you
- Breaking the ice with a new work team or group
- Writing about a key moment in your life for a short, personal, true story
- Generating interview material and topics
- Creating source material to use in The Talk

Pro tip: Humility

(Note: I'm including these pro tips in at the conclusion of story formats where I think they're especially relevant but they should be considered useful across all formats. Some of them even highlight insights into best practice for writing in general.)

One of the keys to telling a great story is to make yourself likable as a storyteller. It can be difficult to do, but it's worth investigating how to do it. This is especially germane in discussing The Maker because The Maker centers on a time when you learned something crucial. When you learn something new it shines a light on the fact that you didn't know something beforehand (or that you thought you understood but really didn't). It's important to admit that. Doing so doesn't make you weak. It makes you more relatable and more likable. Generally speaking, bringing yourself down a few pegs makes the audience care more about you, and in turn, more about your story.

In going about creating this tone in your storytelling, there are several elements that you can include. What does being humble look like in a story? After all, you don't just come out and say that you're humble and consider that box checked. Humility comes through when you're vulnerable, when you admit your fears, take ownership over your mistakes, and recognize your failures. Storytelling is not the place to brag about how clever you were or to play off your failures as intentional or trivial. It's a place to showcase your transformation but only as the endpoint of your struggle. Pointing out where you fell short is not only a good idea, it's essential given what we learned in The Base about how failure fuels every worthwhile story. Laugh at yourself in order to make it sting a little less. Poke fun at yourself and you give the audience a reason to smile. Alongside putting your failures front and center, give credit to others. Being humble means being aware of the fact that everything important that anyone has ever achieved has been a combination of their own insights as well as the groundwork, ideas, and inspiration of those who came before us.

The final note that I'd like to add on likability has to do with pronoun use. You might suggest that this is splitting hairs, but I personally find that the tone-setting implications are wider than they seem at first. If you watch speakers you'll often hear clauses like "I noticed this" or "I realized that" or "I discovered something important." This is technically accurate of course. But to me, a far more effective, humility-establishing pattern is a pattern with "you" at the center instead. So it becomes, "If *you* look at X you'll notice..." or "When *you* stop and think about Y you realize..." or, perhaps the most effective of all, "If *you* go ahead and check out for yourself you'll see that..." Why is this important? Because it's empowering language directed towards the receiver rather than language that spotlights how special or perceptive or curious the speaker is. Perhaps this would not be such an important detail were our species less willing to gravitate towards larger-than-life personalities or gurus professing to have all the answers, individuals who tend to be disempowering over time. Nevertheless, this small detail suggests that you too can come to the same realizations that the speaker did if you lay out the pieces in front of you. It's a small detail, but it says a lot.

The
MAKER

The story that made you who you are.

USS BASE

Universal Story Structure tracks closely with it

TURNING POINT STORY

Focus is on personal life and a key moment that permanently shaped your thinking

SPECIAL — RESOLUTION OR DENOUEMENT

THE END

Emphasizes why the story's events made such a lasting impact and what your new thinking was after it

Story #3 The Vision

The next two stories, The Vision and The Product, have something important in common. They're the two stories among the eight that are unfinished. In other words, some things have happened and some things have yet to happen. The Base provided story material that was all in the past tense. Not here. The Vision is about where a company or organization *could* go. It doesn't have to be a course correction, but it can be that as well. In other words, The Vision can be about addressing things that aren't working or it can be about transforming an organization so that it's fulfilling more of its potential.

Unlike The Base and The Maker, The Vision is not a personal story. It may have elements of personalities in it and will likely start personal, but it's not a main character-centered story like the previous two. It's about assessing and analyzing ideas instead. The Vision questions the status quo solution currently being offered or implemented. It proposes that the solution is too modest or off-target. Since in a story the solution is a product of the problem, The Vision focuses on reinterpreting that problem and thereby inventing a new solution. In other words, The Vision says that we've been mistaken in the way we've been looking at the problem, and if we change the way we see the problem, we change the solution that we could offer. For example, if the market or technology changes, what was once a viable problem/solution pairing for a company may no longer hold. It may be time to recognize that we're now providing an obsolete solution to an outdated problem—and it's time to do something about it.

Since The Base is a main-character driven story format, how does The Vision follow that format yet steer clear of the hero story? We still have exposition. We still have a break in routine. But the revelation is when things start to deviate from the mold. This break in routine leads to a problem, and how important this problem is. Other forces like competitors and government regulations might also come into focus here. These are hints at conflict. The quest is the company's embarking on filling needs. Continued growth and the normal ups and downs of the company or organization represent the complications. However, the complications center on noticing a misfiring between what the needs were at one time and what they are now. The storyteller then shares what he learned from this misalignment, tracking back to the realization that the problem that once was is not the exact same problem any more. To change gears, to put the updated problem front and center instead, will take courage and changes in the way that things are done. But it can be done. It must be done, for reasons A, B, and C. The picture—the vision—of this working is the climax. Following this, is perhaps the most important part of all. It's where the storyteller paints a picture of what things will be like if this reorientation is made, if The Vision is implemented. This is the resolution. In other words whereas The Base said that *because* X happened (climax), Y and Z happened (resolution), The Vision says *if* X happens (climax), Y and Z *can* happen (resolution). With a nod to the typical five-act story structure paradigm, The Vision encapsulates the idea of the hero returning from her moment of insight to share the boon of her new knowledge with the people at large so that they too can benefit.

So The Vision is about leading people to a place they haven't been yet, but providing concrete reasoning as to why this journey is necessary using a story format. It uses the past, present, and future as key components of its structure. The storyteller looks to that past for exposition, break in routine, and initial problem-solving activity. Then the storyteller, instead of explaining what the character is learning as she tries to solve the problem, instead focuses on what she and others have been learning about the current problem-solving activity of the organization, culminating in the conclusion that something has now changed with the underlying conditions or original assessment of the initial problem, which must be reinterpreted. This is all in the present or the very recent past. The final piece is that if we can collectively find the courage to reinterpret the problem and formulate new problem-solving solutions, we can create an even more prosperous trajectory for the organization. This is the future. All three time frames are crucial, because having them all work in concert is what allows The Vision to retain its story structure. So, very generally speaking, The Vision starts with character, moves to ideas, and then ends back with character because the underlying question is whether we have the will, ability, courage, or consensus to see The Vision come true.

Some situations where The Vision is useful:

- Presenting on what you believe the future trajectory of the organization should be

- Presenting when there is not yet empirical evidence of the efficacy of your proposal
- Presenting when there is evidence of alternative models for growth or increased efficiency
- Speaking in a situation where an organization with strong resources and potential is nevertheless struggling with pinpointing its mission
- Concluding data-heavy reports
- Creating a mission statement for an organization

Pro Tip: Interior Story

Don't forget how critical it is that a story has both an internal struggle and an external struggle. This is relevant for every story, but especially for ones like The Vision. The external struggle is the problem in the world that needs solving. We build products (or come up with plans) to solve those problems. The internal struggle is what goes on inside the minds of the people working to make these innovations a reality. In a business story, it's not enough to focus on market forces and economic demand. It's also crucial to pay attention to the people who are trying to keep up, people who are being asked to have the courage to question the status quo and their assumptions about it. This is the human element that takes us from just arranging information and into the realm of story. The emotions, the fight, the human efforts, and the realizations are indispensable elements that move us beyond information.

This internal struggle is supremely important in stories. In character-driven stories, an internal struggle highlights universal themes like love, loyalty, survival, and power that connect at the deepest level with your audience. For concept-driven stories where there is no hero's transformation, internal struggle is equally as important, but just not in the same way. The storyteller is the one that's going to share his internal struggle. How did he feel when he noticed his previous ideas were mistaken? What was his emotional reaction when he realized that the organization needed to adjust its priorities? What were his fears about how others in the organization would respond to this proposal? All of these dimensions of the internal struggle are essential. Truly memorable stories weave the internal and external together as seemingly parallel narratives only to have them touch each other at critical turning points, especially at the critical choice. For The Vision, we move from people (internal), quickly to the heart of the story which is ideas (external), then back to the people who will hopefully make it a reality (internal).

The
VISION

Bringing people where you want them to go.

ONE OF TWO

One of two stories on our list that's unfinished

CRITICAL CHOICE

Here, the critical choice is something that should be made in the future

EMPHASIS #1

The story should not be personal, but rather about ideas

EMPHASIS #2

This story re-looks at the problem and therefore reconsiders the solution

EMPHASIS #3

Past work is applauded and appreciated before new ideas are proposed

Story #4 The Product

Like The Vision, The Product is also a combination of past, present, and hypothetical future events. It also differs in some important ways from The Vision. The Product is in some sense the next logical step beyond The Vision. The Vision lays out what could happen in the future, and The Product is the partial manifestation of that future. The product in question can be an actual thing or a service of course: something that the company or organization could now be offering. The product is formed and ready to go or could be assembled or enacted at any time. Therefore, The Product is essentially a pitch to stakeholders that says we should start selling or offering this product in addition to or in place of what we are already doing.

The structure of The Product, taking a cue from the other stories, starts by selecting material from The Base. Exposition gives us the history of how things have been done. That history also includes deep background which includes action subsections *that happened in the past*, which therefore are all still part of the exposition. Since product and service developments are always in response to new problems (or new perceptions of persistent problems), the revelation of The Product is when a new need is identified and an idea comes into focus about what could satisfy that need. The obstacles represent the brainstorming, experiments, and trials that went into designing and workshoping this new product. And the critical choice centers on whether the company or organization is now going to expand capacity to allow this product to be part of what it offers, arguably a risky endeavour with a potential downside if it fails to work. The resolution is the hypothetical future that's possible if this product is embraced and given the green light.

The key to making The Product work is to acknowledge and appreciate the work that came before, a detail that should also be considered for The Vision. There are two important tendencies about human beings that are worth thinking about here. The first is that they hesitate to change, even when it's change for the better. There are always some people who would rather deal with the devil they know than the angel they don't, people whose sense of "it could be worse" is stronger than a desire to change. The second thing is that when new products are pitched, it's possible for feelings to be hurt. There's an ostensibly knee-jerk reaction to protect your reputation or "turf" and to defend the work that's been done in the past. I think the key to getting the reluctant changers on board is to point out the extreme value that past products have achieved. Ideally, the tone of The Product should not embrace criticism of the past or present (even if it's justified) but to look forward to a new future.

The Product differs from The Vision in one other important way. It's not that The Product is a stronger story, but rather that it just has more ways to make an impression. The Vision is not *entirely* based on trust but there is a significant trust element at play. If there are trust problems between the storyteller and the stakeholders, the way that The Vision is designed mitigates those problems, but yet it doesn't fully eliminate them. After all, The Vision stems from a person's analysis and judgment and if there are concerns about those qualities then those prejudices will influence the story's reception. This is not the case with The Product. The argument for The Product's efficacy should come from data, research, focus-groups, possible competitor success, and from additional sources. In other words, the more ammunition that The Product brings to the table, the less *ad hominem* the presentation is, and arguably the more objectively effective it is. Even a storyteller with trust or credibility problems can tell The Product and be convincing as long as the evidence is sound and in place.

Some situations where The Product is useful:

- Introducing a product, prototype, or concrete idea for an object or service that should be promoted by your company or organization but currently isn't
- Presenting to a group of potential investors
- Presenting to a group of prospective partners needed to finalize making the product or idea a reality
- Creating sales team exercises and training materials

Pro Tip: Show Don't Tell

It's nearly impossible to go to a class, workshop, lecture, or seminar on writing without hearing the mantra "show don't tell." But what does it actually mean? Show don't tell means that the most effective and satisfying storytelling for adults allows the story receivers to connect the dots themselves, to draw conclusions about what's happening without being directly told. I added adults because in children's writing or YA (young adult) literature there's nothing wrong at all with writing, "She was nervous," or "The beach was calm and serene." Those are forms of telling but they're expected in that genre. For adults, they're less welcome. The more you can show, the better. Showing means telling the audience that she was looking at her watch and tapping her foot while wiping sweat off her brow instead of saying she was nervous. Showing means talking about the way the palm trees are barely moving as the morning sun glints off of them to show that the beach is calm and serene. In other words, paint the picture and let the audience render judgement.

Since an underlying assumption for the eight stories I'm detailing here is that they will be told to adults, show don't tell is highly relevant. Whether it's The Product or other stories, it's problematic to say that a product is cutting-edge, or dynamic, or multi-faceted. Those adjectives are for infomercials. Instead, use studies and information to show the audience how impressive something is. Show them the concrete ways that people's lives will be improved. The introduction of a new product or service is a huge addition for any company or organization. A lot may be at stake. Subjective telling is not compelling. Raw numbers and impact assessments are. This is a super important point. All along in this book I've been saying that stories are more than information. They are, it's true, but stories do *include* information. The skeleton is not the body but the muscles, organs, and nerves need the skeleton to stay together. In this case, we can see the interplay between information, knowledge, and wisdom. Let information do what it's good at when the time is right. Build the story around those data punctuations to complete the picture, assembling a mountain of evidence that leads to the change moment.

The
PRODUCT

Introducing a new game-changing offering.

ONE OF TWO

One of two stories on our list that's unfinished

REVELATION

Realization of a need that that this organization or company can address

COMPLICATIONS

Research and trials to find a solution until breakthrough

CLIMAX

Product proposal or reveal

RESOLUTION

Implications of this product or service's potential to transform

Story #5 The Springboard

The Springboard is a story format proposed by author Stephen Denning, one of the business storytelling field's most prominent voices. He makes a very strong case for the merits of this story in the aptly titled *The Leader's Guide to Storytelling*. I'll provide a condensed version of his format, but I would highly recommend reading his entire text for the full level of detail. I'm going to spend a little extra time getting into the nuances of this story format because of how different it is to the stories I've discussed so far.

The Springboard is a story where you tell someone else's story from the past as an illustration of a change that a specific audience should implement in their work. It's called The Springboard because the purpose of the story is to inspire (or spring) people to action, which is far more effective than simply asking them to drop the way they've done things and to start doing something new. It provides a critically important missing element, which is a set of best practice tips when it comes to telling another person's story most effectively.

Here are the four most important things to keep in mind when telling The Springboard:

- Make sure the change idea is crystal clear
- Make sure the protagonist is typical of (or similar to) the audience
- Make sure the story is told in minimalist fashion

- Make sure to articulate what would have happened in the past were the change/s not implemented

Let's go deeper into each one of these.

The change idea means the exact change that you're trying to instigate in the present by telling this story about the past. It's easy to point out what's wrong in an organization and all the ramifications of those problems. It's more challenging to pinpoint exactly what change is necessary. But it's critical because there can be no disconnect between the change at the heart of the story you're telling and the change you are hoping to see implemented. In other words, the audience should see a direct line between what changed in the story and what can change in the specific environment around them right now. If they can't, then the story may still have some value but it will miss its mark as it goes into a mental file for the audience, irrelevant for the situation at hand. Whether it's client response time, efficiency of information sharing, marketing innovation, or anything else, the in-house identified change being proposed must match the story example change being shared.

It's very important that the audience be able to identify with the character/s at the center of The Springboard. Remember, the idea here is that the story will serve as inspiration for your audience to make a similar change. So the more in alignment—with respect to the field and the level—between the story's context and your audience's context, the stronger potential success for the story. For example, if you're advocating change for senior managment, ensure that your story example also centers on senior management. It's important to remember that people rarely want to change. It's a natural thing to resist. Combine that with fragile personalities and you could have a powder keg where people feel "attacked" by simply suggesting that what they're doing is not perfect already. As frustrating as this might be, it happens. As a storyteller, you want to reduce the possibility, as much as you can, of your audience thinking, *Sure, for those people in that industry doing that kind of work, that might have helped. But it will never work for us.* Searching for the right story where your audience and your characters are in similar positions helps prevent that short-circuiting. Not just any story will do.

Tell the story in a minimalist fashion. I recommend that all stories told in a business setting be told as efficiently as possible, with few detours and extra embellishments, but with The Springboard, it's important to be *especially* barebones. The reason for this is that the more minimal it is, the more it invites the listeners to fill in the gaps with their own details. This is critical because the end purpose is for the story to become *their* story in the end. Stories told for other purposes are often about showing you what life is like in someone else's shoes. Here, the idea is to get the listener to put those shoes on herself. The more skeltal, the more the listener can put her own layers of personal specifics onto the story, to adapt it to her context, and to find a way to put forward solutions to her specific needs. It's counter-intuitive in the traditional storytelling world to tell a story this way, but for adults in The Springboard story's unique context, this style makes the act of storytelling as participatory as possible, increasing the chances that your listeners will attempt to personalize it. If someone feels like a story is theirs, and not just someone else's, their willingness to attempt change is more likely and, therefore, the possibility of organizational transformation is more likely too.

Make sure to say what would have happened if the change in the story didn't take place. As we'll discuss more in the harvesting section in the final chapter of this book, it's important to find stories where the stakes are high. In other words, if the purpose of telling the story in the first place is the inspirational change element, then the final detail must be what its absence would have cost. It's not being negative to do so, but being realistic; it speaks to how the change in the story altered the trajectory of how things were going. It's the final piece of evidence that bolsters just how valuable the story's change was for those who made it as well as how valuable it continues to be for those who can make it in other companies (like the one you're presenting to).

One final note on The Springboard. If you think about it, The Springboard and The Vision are not too far apart. The typical Springboard suggests by looking at these certain events that happened in the past we can draw these conclusions and adopt a like-minded plan for our organization. So if we learn lessons from A, we can do what A did. But what if you want to tell a story that goes beyond that to say that we can learn a lesson from A and do what A did, *but once we've done A we can also extend that to B and even possibly C?* That's taking The Springboard and combining it with The Vision—and it's a powerful combination. Embrace the idea that once you see how each of the story models work on their own, you can play with linking them and making something even more closely tailor-made to the needs of the moment.

Some situations where The Springboard is useful:

- Providing an example of another person or company's story where something was changed that you would like to see changed in your organization as well
- Consulting with other companies and organizations looking to learn from successes of the past
- Creating source material to use in hybrid with The Vision

Pro Tip: For the Springboard, keep the details down except for three

There is one key element to The Springboard that was not mentioned above. I discussed the strategic importance of telling the story in a minimalist way in order to encourage the audience to fill in their own personal details and build the story world themselves (including inserting themselves in it). But there are three seemingly small details that are in fact very important to include and not to omit in the spirit of minimalism: the time, the place, and the main character's name of the story from the past. As we learned with exposition, these details might even be communicated in a single sentence: "So let me take you back to

Geneva in 2003 at the office of Avinash Kumar." And that's it. We never have to mention a date or a place or a name ever again in the story. Why is this so important? Because it instantly creates credibility. One of the absolute core properties of The Springboard is that every single thing that you say about what happened at this previous company or organization must be true. An instant way to communicate that to the audience is to give certain specifics. It implies that your story is genuine and indirectly suggests to your audience that if they were to check the facts of the story themselves (which some undoubtedly will do) they will find it to be accurate. Just three little elements, but they pack an incredibly important punch. Note, as we will discuss in a later pro tip, there might not be any one person who is at the center of the story you're telling. If that's the case then there is no need to name the person at all. You can refer to the position or the office or the team as the change agent in the story.

Interestingly, this is, again, one of the points that makes The Springboard different from the other stories in this book. Details and nuances are important for the other seven stories, and very often those details can make the story come alive for the audience. When you're painting a picture for someone, those details are memorable. But here in The Springboard the purpose of the story is not to take a fine brush to the story world but to push forward to and showcase the change agent and the change moment, intentionally leaving the story black and white in order to stay hyper focused on the story's purpose. It's not about getting the audience to viscerally feel a place, but rather about a clear and concrete lesson to be learned from someone else's example.

Denning correctly suggests that while storytelling is fun, the understandable impulse to entertain while telling The Springboard will work against you and will only weaken the story. Therefore the end product looks quite different from what other models lead us to expect, but that speaks not to what makes a "good" story, but instead to just how high of a priority the business lesson at the heart of The Springboard actually is.

The
SPRINGBOARD

Using another person's story to propose change.

WHAT IF

Core is someone else's story with the key question: "What if we did something like that?"

1 LEARNING

At least one main thing that you, the storyteller, took from this story

MINIMAL BUT ACCURATE

When telling this particular story the details should be minimal but fully accurate

COMPARE & CONTRAST

Articulate the differences and similarities between your situation and the story's

VISION/HYBRID

It's Ok to share your thoughts on your organization's future beyond implementing this change

Story #6 The Morale Builder

Storytelling isn't always about pitching new products or ideas. It's not merely a great way to introduce yourself to others that you'll be working with. It's also incredibly useful in situations where a human connection is needed. As the name of this story suggests, a story can be a confidence-building (or repairing) mechanism. When cohesiveness or cooperation dips, it can be an invaluable tool to put things back on track.

In a story, things that happen are followed by introspection. In other words, events occur and then the character reacts to those events and comes up with some kind of plan to remedy or alter the problem that is coming into focus. This is the typical pattern in any story. For The Morale Builder, we all but mute the things that happen and elevate the introspection. So the story is flush with humanity, if you will, instead of the action/reaction back and forth.

The three elements to put front and center in The Morale Builder relate to the climax and resolution. The first is a change moment for the storyteller at the organization. So this refers to either the positive insight or positive change in circumstance that the storyteller experienced followed by going back and unpacking how that came about. The remaining two elements are both part of the resolution. The first reminds the audience what it is that the company or organization does and how they are helping to make the world a better place. In other words, reminding them how important the work is that they do. And the second resolution-based element entailes sharing some powerful customer or stakeholder anecdotes that reiterate the value of the company, its brand, and its output. So just to summarize: key personal change moment, then the important work this company is doing, followed by examples and impressions from stakeholders.

So with The Morale Builder, the focus is constantly on broadening out, beyond just the workplace, which can sometimes be filled with over-fixation on minutia, petty arguments, and even personal rivalry. Whether those specific elements are present or not, the key is to push out and away from the everyday details of the workspace and to shift the focus to the broad human and social implications of the work being done at this specific company. The larger context. The storyteller uses personal, small moments that had a major impact on him to bridge that gap and to take the story towards that big picture.

Beyond just workplace friction, The Morale Builder is also useful when larger, existential events cast a shadow on a company's survival prospects. Things like financial crises, military turmoil, terrorist aftermath, and viral pandemics can decimate even the most positive and efficient workplaces. The Morale Builder is a strong antidote to those forces, mitigating their potentially devastating impact. It reminds those affected that problems don't last forever even if it seems that way.

Keep in mind that this structure that I'm proposing here constitutes the broad strokes and the foci needed to achieve this story format's larger purpose. Like The Base, it's possible to play with the order and elements of the Morale Builder and still make the story work. For example, it's possible to share someone else's change moment in the company and how this came about, with the storyteller ending the story noting how he's noticed the same thing in his own work and experience. In other words, you can switch the change agent or move the client feedback anecdotes to the beginning as long as the storyteller caps it off with personal first-hand confirmation of that sentiment. Experimenting is key to finding the right way to make these story templates work for you. These elements need not be fixed in stone. Once you understand their larger purpose, you can consider what else could be just as effective.

Some situations where The Morale Builder is useful:

- Speaking to a group of people in need of a pep talk or positivity
- Dispelling divisive office politics
- Countering an atmosphere where negativity has become a strong distraction
- Encouraging a frustrated workforce to persevere under adverse working conditions
- Providing talking points for HR teams dealing with unexpected turnover

Pro Tip: Don't focus on the villain

This pro tip is especially relevant to The Morale Builder but it's important beyond just this story. The Morale Builder must be focused on positivity. Yes, the reasons for workplace discord come from bad habits and unaddressed behavior that deserve attention at some point—but that's for another day. The Morale Builder is intended to concentrate on the best of our natures. Because of that, my strong advice is to steer clear of focusing on antagonists, negative influences, and villains. Again, are they important? Yes. But they're counter-productive in terms of the purpose of telling this particular story. It will work against you rather than provide clarity and inspiration.

While antagonists are certainly key parts of stories at large, they should not be a remotely significant part of any of the eight story formats outlined in this book. In addition to it being a professional taboo to openly demonize someone in a presentation, the person is not there to defend themselves. Plus, it's not necessary. Even when a crucial part of the story is the actions of another person, it's far more effective to couch those actions as a "different point of view" or "bad luck" or to use it as a way to turn the focus back onto the main character, whether it's you or someone else. A very powerful work-around is to say that "obstacles presented themselves" that forced you to relook at the situation and to come up with a new strategy to move forward. That's exactly what reaction the villain instigates, so concentrate on the reaction rather than the cause. You can communicate that with absolute clarity without ever having to get down into personal naming, even when it might be justified. As The Morale Builder calls for positivity above all else, avoiding settling old scores in a presentation keeps the integrity of the story intact. Your audience will appreciate your storytelling taking the high road.

The
MORALE BUILDER

Giving those around you a jolt of inspiration.

EXPOSITION FOCUS 1

What makes us unique as an organization

EXPOSITION FOCUS 2

Big picture: How we're helping people and the world

CLIMAX

Key change moment for you at this organization

RESOLUTION

Powerful customer/client anecdotes

Story #7 The Capsule

The Capsule is probably the most unique of all the eight formats in this collection. Another name for The Capsule would be The Elevator Pitch. How do you tell your whole story when you only have about a minute to do it? The bad news is that you can't. But the good news is that you can use highlights from The Base to get as close as possible to an effective story structure in the small amount of time that you do have. Here's how it's done.

All of the pieces of the universal story structure outlined in The Base are crucial. As I've been discussing, take one piece out and the ripple effects reverberate out into the entire structure. However, I also noted that some pieces seem to be of elevated importance. You can consider these the key turning points in a story's structure. The two moments that we've put more emphasis on than any others so far have been the revelation and the critical choice. So the way to build The Capsule is to include those elements and to build essentially a proto-story (which is not quite a story) around those two, adding three important others along the way.

The Capsule starts with the routine. Remember, as fairy tales taught us, the routine does not need to be a ton of material. Sometimes it's just one line. We move from that routine to the revelation starting with a quick break in routine that is then immediately shown to be significant. The problem immediately grows out of that. The trials (or attempts to solve the problem) are summarized until we get to the key crystallization of the concept which is where the critical choice is. The change moment of

119

insight or circumstance is when the product, service, or idea is implemented or conceived. The change created by this should be explicitly stated and not implied. And the resolution is the impact this will have on the market, the community, or people's lives more broadly. Under this abbreviated format, you can hit the highlights and the key turning points in a matter of seconds rather than minutes. Is it better to tell your full story, complete with the struggles, setbacks, initial misperceptions, self-doubt, and breakthrough? Always. But it just might be a luxury that you don't have.

One important thing to note is that the routine itself might *already* be the problem. This is often the case with inventions and other products. In other words, the way things are done now (the routine) is inefficient and frustrating. The revelation then becomes a realization of how to improve efficiency and remove frustration. This way of formatting the story turns the revelation into more of a challenge born of the exposition rather than a realization of a problem stemming from the break in routine. This is fine. Although I have not touched on it so far, an expanded way of looking at the story problem, even in the universal story structure, encompasses more than just fixing something that's gone wrong. It also can involve freeing stakeholders from a burden or embarking on an incentive-laden adventure. In this expanded way of looking at this element, the mission of the story is not simply always exactly solving a problem, but can also be the challenge of finding the route to a reward. The mission becomes accomplishing a high-stakes task and the problem is now exactly how best to carry out the mission.

If this is confusing at all, here it is in a nutshell. For The Capsule to work, it needs two pieces: a universal theme and a change moment. How exactly does the universal theme emerge? It emerges out of a problem that all of us (or a huge slice of us) face, have faced, or could face. This is the problem that that revelation brings to light (as a result of the routine or break in routine). How can we solve this problem? By changing something. In the spirit of brevity that The Capsule prioritizes, perhaps the most effective way to articulate change is a rethink using "what if." So the storyteller responds to the universal problem by essentially saying something like, "Maybe we've been thinking about this all wrong. What if we did X instead of Y." So while we can unpack the details, the two anchors of The Capsule are simply the universal theme and the rethink. With those two cadences, The Capsule will always be on solid footing. When those two are identified, the most important work is already done.

Some situations where The Capsule is useful:

- Presenting when time is very short, like an "elevator pitch" scenario
- Brainstorming for marketing purposes when considering what should be emphasized for a short video or commercial script
- Preparing for an interview where time is limited

Pro Tip: Who is the main character?

The Capsule brings up something that's useful to think about. The Capsule's unique circumstances—the very limited amount of time that you have to hit the highlights of your story—forces you to do some things and to make some choices that you might not otherwise make. We've said before that humility is one of the keys to telling a strong story and ensuring likeability, and that one of those keys is spreading the credit. We've also learned in the pro tip from The Springboard, how important it is to get your facts and your details correct, including the names of people involved. However, The Capsule's constraints can override these details and make them gratuitous. Therefore two things can come into play.

One is combining everyone that you might be working with into "we." In most enterprises, whether it's a new start-up or an established organization, there is a group of people who have different roles, but in The Capsule, there very well may be no time for those details. So "we" or "our team" are perfectly acceptable ways to depict your side of things. Likewise, if someone else's story is involved, say for example a key moment in your version of The Capsule involves some other company's team, you may have to collapse all of the key players down into one person—maybe the head of the team. The story receiver knows you have very little time and she knows that summarizing is a necessity, so it's not being deceptive to do this. It's efficient. So instead of person A did this, while person B added this, and then they collaborated with person C who got approval from person D (all of which may be the complete truth), it becomes just one person who did it. This one person decided to act. This one person took a risk. And because this one person took a risk, here's how it paid off. This bending of the truth under these abnormal storytelling conditions is perfectly fair play.

There are other observations that we can make about this pro tip beyond the context of The Capsule. Sometimes in stories, especially when the protagonists (or heroes) are a group of people, it's hard to pinpoint the main character. But why should we try to do it anyway? Because the main character is the one who will be responsible for the critical choice and the corresponding risk that comes with it. So in the design of the story how can you identify the main character? One way is that the main character will be the one with the needy ghosts. But if that's too abstract, another way to identify her will be that she's the one who changes the most. In a duo or trio of central characters, they will usually all change in some way at the climax, but the one whose personality and worldview changes the most is the main character. It's very possible in story writing that this realization might come after an initial draft of the climax and will cause the storyteller to go back and to attribute the critical choice to the character he now realizes is in fact the main character. Story design is a process of trial and error, almost never something that happens all at once on the first try.

The
CAPSULE

Abbreviated version of a story using 5 pivotal plot points.

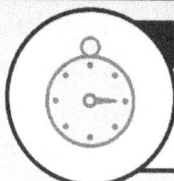

ROUTINE
Establishment of the normal world

REVELATION
Realization of the problem

CRITICAL CHOICE
Rethink needed, leads to risk and action

CHANGE
Explicitly stated rather than implied

IMPLICATIONS
What the change will mean, ripple effects

124

The Talk refers to the exciting phenomenon that the TED organization has mainstreamed in the last few decades. TED, TEDx, and inspired spinoffs have allowed innovative thinkers and exceptional presenters to reach entirely new audiences with their ideas and work. The sheer magnitude of topics that these platforms explore is breathtaking. And the excitement around them forces us, in a sense, to consider how this format intersects with storytelling. Obviously I think it does, which is why I included it in this book. Looking closer at this, there are some observations that we can make that are work investigating.

First, not all TED-style talks are stories. Many are demonstrations or even performances with explanation. They are sometimes mini-lectures or masterclasses where a concept is introduced and a lesser-known detail about something is highlighted. Any of these can be powerful. Yet, over time, one noticeable feature of these talks is how much more story-like they've become. Even in presentations that are academic or artistic, they tend to be bookended by stories, a pattern that makes sense when you see how much TED coaching materials dovetail with the universal story structure.

Having said that, TED-style talks are almost never *entirely* stories. And this is the crux of why The Talk has its own category here in this book. The purpose is not to simply tell a personal story or to focus on the transformative turning point in it. It's also not just designed to simply provide a product demo, to tell someone else's story, or to build morale. It is those things but something *more* too. The Talk, in my view, uses storytelling to provide the context into what led the speaker towards a breakthrough of some kind and then—and this is the important part—what the larger, real-world implications are for this ideological breakthrough. In a way, it borrows elements from The Springboard but rather than exploring how the change elements will benefit a single company or organization, The Talk is focused on how the change element will impact the world.

So with The Talk there is an ending that focuses on the big picture and imagining what would happen if this idea being discussed were more widespread. What is it about this invention, organization, reconsideration, or discovery of what previously went unrealized that could have wide-reaching implications across a number of fields? What does this breakthrough mean for how we see ourselves and our potential? Does this insight have ramifications that could lead to a more peaceful planet or a reduction of unnecessary suffering where it currently exists? These are some of the big questions that resonate at the end of The Talk. The size of these questions does not come into play in any of our other formats and therefore, it's critical to acknowledge this unique and exciting story. The only story that is in fact preoccupied with the big picture is The Morale Builder. But that's the only thing that that format and The Talk have in common. The pattern in The Talk is a personal story with a transition to potentially mainstream implications (not just changes for one specific company).

Some situations where The Talk is useful:

- Presenting in a large innovation and creative thinking forum
- International diplomacy and other endevous with widespread, even global, dimensions
- Providing an opening or closing statement to a jury

Pro tip: Bookending

While it's not always possible, bookending is an incredibly satisfying story structure detail. Bookending simply refers to returning to something at the end that was introduced at the beginning of the story. The two most common bookending targets are locations and words.

Let's look at these a little closer. To bookend with a location, the story starts off with a location as part of the exposition. Exposition, as discussed above, is part of the everyday, normal world. Then the story, the adventure, breaks off from that. Making our way through the stages of the action sequence and then to the climax, we eventually come to the resolution, the new normal. It's very often the case that the location that we learned about in the exposition still in fact exists even in the realm of this new normal. Bookending would be where the main character now returns back to that place but with a new understanding, a new insight because of what was transformed over the course of the story. But a strong talk need not always involve a physical adventure. It can just be an adventure of the mind, where something as simple as a word or phrase now takes on new meaning in the wake of a story. In line with this, a storyteller might end her story by noting that now, "whenever she hears the word X, she thinks something very different," something that the events of the story made possible.

Bookending is worth noting not only for its aesthetic appeal but because, arguably, the first and last moments of a story are the most important given how critical they are tied with an audience's first impression and the echo of a closing statement. It's a go-to strategy for ending that exudes hope and the sentimental tones that make The Talk so resonant.

The
TALK

Formatting your story for a conference presentation.

BEST OF BOTH

Make your presentation into a speech/story hybrid

WIDE SCOPE

Most resembles The Maker but can include elements of many story formats

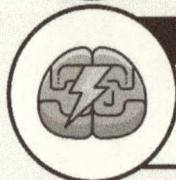

BREAKTHROUGH MOMENT

Climax is breakthrough moment of change in insight

END WITH BIG Qs

Close by posing the big questions and challenges ahead

HOPE

End on a tone that has a strong sense of hope

Closing Thoughts on the 8 Stories

This closes out the section on the eight stories that businesses and professionals will need. As you can see, each of them takes the raw material from The Base, and then strips away certain parts while spotlighting others. I hope you feel invited to use these templates to create stories of your own, noticing that subtle emphases can make a huge difference when it comes to targeting your message. I hope you also have a sense, as I mentioned in the opening, that a presentation is not synonymous with a story. Presentation is the larger of the two. In other words, for a full presentation you very well might be looking to put together story and non-story material. Not everything must be in a story format to be communicated effectively. Keep the hybrid as a target rather than feeling pressure to make sure everything is covered under the umbrella of a story.

As any sculptor at a pottery wheel knows, I would strongly suggest putting more clay in front of you than you'll eventually need. In other words, use The Base to see the full story (and tangents) and then shape that clay according to your specific needs. While it's important to be confident, don't be overconfident and go into this work with tunnel vision. Seeing all the options in front of you keeps you from preemptively cutting off story pathways simply because they didn't immediately occur to you. The more choices you have the better, especially because not every story will work. Like story writing itself, picking the right story for the right moment is a dance of trial and error as well as soul searching. These things take time. The story, and the story's fit with your needs, will be stronger if you don't rush. The greatest insights have a way of coming out when they're ready, not necessarily when we're ready.

CHAPTER 4 - HARVESTING

Sourcing Clay

Harvesting means finding stories. We've been looking at the different ways to shape the clay. Now it's time to talk about where to find it, how to source the material that you'll use to build your stories. It's slightly more challenging than it sounds, especially because of the popular misunderstanding of what a story is. Even though we're learning what a story is and isn't, the overstretched version of the term is like the air that we breathe: we can't ignore it and we can't escape from it. And it affects what comes to mind when we first think of the subject matter for a story we want to tell.

Some of the stories from our list have an obvious topic built into them. Specifically, the impetus to tell The Vision and The Product come from the need to find a way to convey that specific information. You have a hope for what your company can do, so you arrange the ideas into The Vision format. You have an innovative campaign that you believe should be a new centerpiece to what your organization offers, so you use The Product format.

But the other stories' subject matter is not so straight-forward. For The Maker, you want to find a story that focuses on circumstances that changed your personal character. For The Springboard, you want to find a story from history, ideally from the field or sector that your organization is in, to serve as a model that can be learned from. For The Morale Builder, you're looking for something from the past that made a personal, local, positive impact, that will help turn things around. For The Talk, you're looking for a moment of character building that also could change the world. And of course The Capsule is just a condensed version of one of these. Looking at these five, we can see that there are hundreds of topics that you can pick that can lead to the desired outcome. So how do you choose? What makes for rich story material? When you have multiple options for core ideas, what makes certain ones stand apart as the better choices around which to build stories?

Before getting into some specifics, I just want to offer a word of caution. Many of us, including me, have our go-to stories. These are the stories we tell on a regular basis: at cocktail parties, at professional functions, at conferences, and among friends. We know these stories by heart and can tell them at the drop of a hat. So when I say that it's important to do some story harvesting, you might feel like it's not necessary because you already have a set of stories that you know people respond to. However, it is very likely that this is the first time that you're reading about The Base in such detail. Add to that the fact that many, though not all, of our go-to stories are meant to lighten the mood or to entertain. The stories this book is helping you to create do not have entertainment as their primary goal. They use the details of The Base and modify them depending on the exact situation at hand to take on serious issues. It's very unlikely that a story you already have will check those boxes. But even if it does, and even if the stories you use now are wide-ranging and highly effective, recognize that you have far more stories than you might think. The tagline for my company, Tall Tales, is "Everyone has at least one great story." But in truth, everyone has about ten great stories. They just might not realize it. So go into this harvesting work assuming that you have more stories than you think you do. With an open mind, you give yourself permission to explore and meander into the corners of your life that you didn't even know you remembered.

Let's explore some of the characteristics to consider when it comes to finding strong story topics for all the stories aside from the special cases of The Vision and The Product. Included here are also several key things to consider once you've found a topic and are starting to shape it.

Come up with a list of several stories before picking the one you're going with.

The first practical step should involve jotting down many possible ideas that you have for stories. Just like rough drafts of a piece of writing, it's Ok if these are sloppy and full of holes. More specifically, there should be a mix of great ideas and not so great ideas. It's absolutely incredible the way that the brain works sometimes and how bad ideas can provide the precisely needed stepping stones to breakthroughs. Moreover, many times the bad ideas are actually pointing you in a very useful direction, but their angle is just slightly off. Every single idea that you come up with is useful in its own way and the more you come up with, the more options you have. Don't stop simply because you found something excellent. Keep going, discover more, continue to dig, and you will find far more useful material than you would have ever initially thought.

Look for stories where the stakes are high.

I can't stress how important this is. High stakes means that by the time the full extent of the problem is revealed, the consequences of not solving the problem loom very large. When the stakes are high, tension is naturally built into a story because of how much you have to lose if this situation doesn't go your way. The key to doing this is to build up the value of the thing that is about to be put under threat. When that happens, the audience now knows what losing this would mean and is rooting for you to be successful. When the stakes are low, the air is sucked out of a story. The audience has no emotional investment in the outcome. (The exception for this is funny stories where the reason the story is funny in the first place is because something of small consequence is being treated like a huge problem by one of the characters. The audience sticks with you as voyeurs to the absurdity in order to be entertained by the fix's elusive proximity.) The overwhelming amount of stories in a business setting will not be told for entertainment value but for communicating heartfelt sentiments and concrete actionable lessons.

Find stories that involve reconsidering conventional wisdom or "obvious" facts.

When we explored the catastrophe and the critical choice in The Base, we discussed how complex those moments are. Taking a break from the fight, from the main character's perspective, is seemingly the beginning of their admitting defeat. But yet in that time of reflection, all kinds of things become possible that were once too theoretical for the character to focus on. He's been trying to put out fires constantly up until this point. He's had no time to truly reflect on (or process) this entire sequence of events. But when he finally gets that chance, he starts to question everything. He questions his role in all of this and whether his instinct in refusing the call at the start was in fact correct after all. He questions the insights that he's learned as he overcame initial complications and obstacles. But his questions also go deeper. He starts to question the very nature of how he sees himself in the world, his worldview. He looks at who he was, who he is, and who he wants to be. And he starts to look at what's preventing him from being who he wants to be. In this moment, everything is now on the table in terms of reconsideration. He's now not only free to, but encouraging himself to, reinterpret the history, values, and so-called common sense that he's never questioned before. Suddenly he realizes that addressing this inner turmoil propells him to make the critical choice and to give the story mission one final try.

Bringing this back to a business storytelling context, the catastrophe and critical choice provide the opportunity to question conventional wisdom. Just because something has been done a certain way doesn't mean that it always must be done that way. Just because something is controversial doesn't mean it's incapable of producing the necessary result. And, perhaps most importantly, just because something has not been tried before, doesn't mean it should remain untried. Stories that involve this kind of rethinking and reinterpretation of tradition are especially powerful stories. Audiences love the exposé, the short-hand term for revealing the deeper character of something we thought we already understood. Looking at something with "fresh eyes" free of the burden of previous judements might just be they key to unlocking your entire story.

Don't tell someone else's story except for The Springboard.

This is especially a problem for new storytellers. New storytellers will often solve the problem of having to delve into their own pasts, psyches, and fears by avoiding it all together and telling someone else's story. Telling someone else's story is a perfectly acceptable form of storytelling. But not in the business storytelling context aside from The Springboard. Whether it's The Maker, The Talk, or The Capsule, one of the goals of telling the story in the first place is for the audience to learn more about you, not someone else. Therefore, it requires that you are the main character of the story. If, perhaps, there is some ambiguity because you're in fact in the story but so is someone else, the question arises as to who the main character is. As we noted earlier, the main character is the character who changes the most. In The Springboard, that's *supposed* to be another person (and their corresponding organization). But in The Maker, The Talk, and The Capsule, that spotlight should be shone on you. For The Vision, The Product, and The Morale Builder however, the change is not a change in insight inside a person but a change in circumstances that can result from looking at things differently and altering the status quo. These latter three still are personal stories with you heavily involved, but the change is not necessarily a personal one. Nuances aside, seven of our eights stories should be focused on you. There is nothing that even comes close to the power of sharing a part of yourself with an audience.

Key considerations when you're shaping the story

So you have some stories and now it's time to work on them. It's time to unpack them, to tease them out, to see what's under the surface, what they might be connected to, and what the strongest ways to build them entail. There are also some other factors to consider.

Make sure there isn't a huge piece of context that you're leaving out.

This is most important for The Springboard but it's a major consideration for the other stories too. In discussing why you did something or why some other organization did something, it's possible that massive situational realities were the real determining factors and not the specific decisions that were made that you're focusing on. This is called spurious reasoning: when two things happen in sequence and we draw the conclusion that they must have a cause and effect relationship. For example, if you're telling the story of a company that went under due to poor choices in 2008 or 2020 but you fail to mention the global financial crisis or the COVID-19 outbreak, respectively, then the story loses its punch. The failure of that business venture might have actually had nothing to do with poor organizational decisions. It's still possible to tell a story under these circumstances, and there is of course always an influential context even without a worldwide recession or pandemic, but you must take it into account in the story so that it doesn't overshadow the events you're placing under the microscope. If it goes unmentioned, your listeners will focus on the outer context, not what happened inside that. The only way to avoid audience preoccupation with the big picture is to address it head on.

It's Ok to have no circumstantial change as long as there is a dramatic change in insight.

Remember the change element that I discussed in the opening chapter and that I have been reiterating. Every story must involve change—but there are different kinds of changes. The Big Three are change in circumstance, change in insight, and change in relationship. This is worth revisiting here for a second. Imagine that you're considering telling a story in a business setting. But as you unpack and outline the events of the story you realize that in the end, the key decision to move the company in a new direction was't taken. Instead of changing focus, the company decided to refocus on what they were currently doing but with more creativity and efficiency. Is there a problem here, story-wise? Absolutely not. This is a perfect example where the change in circumstance does not in fact occur, but a new way of thinking develops instead. Change in insight is enough to hold up an entire story. Don't be afraid of exploring it because it feels like "nothing happened." Very often things are happening, but they're not visible changes so we discount them at first.

Ensure that it's a one-way presentation. Save interactivity for a different time.

It may seem obvious but the reason this reminder is so important is because it cuts against conventional wisdom about best-practice in a presentation. Often at certain moments, getting input and feedback from the receivers can be important, not only as a way of keeping them engaged but also acknowledging their value (especially in a team atmosphere). But the impulse to include participation must be fought. While your audience will likely react at certain moments, a story is not a conversation, but a magnification of one person's experience. We point that spotlight at this specific series of events in order to draw insight and conclusions beyond just those events. Your audience *wants* to give you the spotlight and they want to learn from you. Anytime that focus is shifted for any significant length of time, the less impact your story will have. After your story is finished is the perfect time for interaction or questions and answers, not during.

Practicing is part of the harvesting process. You *must* practice.

And lastly, if harvesting is a process of coming up with story material and preparing it for delivery, then practicing should be included in the latter part of that process. Unfortunately, I have seen and worked with many enthusiastic storytellers who nevertheless failed to give any previous thought to their stories prior to telling them. The reasoning was that since they've told them before and lived the experience, they assumed that it's all in their heads and can simply be accessed like opening a drawer in a filing cabinet. Only the absolute most experienced storytellers can do this, and even some of them can't. To tell your story the best that you can involves practice. A lot of it. To yourself, to a mirror, or to a friend. If you're afraid that too much practice will ruin the spontaneity, remember what actors do. They rehearse something to create the illusion of spontaneity. They don't ignore their lines until filming because they want to capture the energy of the moment. Rehearsal is critical. And if the best storytellers in the world have to rehearse then that means all of us should be rehearsing.

A final word on harvesting

Keep in mind one important aspect of harvesting. If you've read this book and now feel confident to start to scan your memories and experience for stories, then that's fantastic. If you're also thinking about working with others to do this, then that's great too, but, keep in mind that when you do this, you will also have to find a way to teach them what a story is in the first place. *You* know what one is, just like you now know how to conceptualize, visualize, then build and refine a house. But, given what we have repeated over and over again about how our zeitgeist defines the word "story," you will be confronting others' misunderstanding at every turn. In fact, to harvest stories with others effectively, some preparation will likely be necessary. It can be couched as a set of guidelines or a pre-harvesting pep talk, but whatever form it comes in, your ability to mine organizations and groups for stories will be immeasurably more successful when those individuals understand what stories actually are.

HARVESTING

Tips for selecting stories:

Come up with a list of several stories before picking the one you're going with.

Look for stories where the stakes are high.

Find stories that involve reconsidering conventional wisdom or "obvious" facts.

Don't tell someone else's story except for The Springboard.

Tips for refining stories after selection:

Make sure there isn't a huge piece of context that you're leaving out.

It's Ok to have no circumstance change as long as there is a dramatic change in insight.

Ensure that it's a one-way presentation. Save interactivity for a different time.

Conclusion

Storytelling has been a victim of its own success. Here's why I say that. Over the last twenty-plus years, people from every sector of society have realized its immense value. From the catharsis and humor of live storytelling to experiments in all kinds of short and micro fiction. From organizational storytelling fundraising strategies to brand reinvention through narrative design, storytelling is an essential ingredient in selling, marketing, and most importantly, remembering. So what's the problem? The problem is that as storytelling's profile and stature has grown, so have its dimensions as a slice of communication overall. Remember Venn diagrams from science class in high school? Communication is a massive circle, and while storytelling is also a massive circle, they are two different circles that overlap. But as pop culture has elevated the importance of storytelling, its circle has started to move into communication's so much so that ideas like "everything is a story" and "all writing is storytelling" do not sound as outlandish as they should sound. In fact, such phrases have a friendly, all-inclusive ring to them that makes them appealing. And yet if everything is a story then how do we become better storytellers? By studying and practicing "everything"? I don't think so.

A story is actually a specific thing. It's a certain kind of communication, an arrangement that has noticeable patterns and characteristics. Far from dogmatically limiting and thus reducing the potential of stories, defining what a story is frees you from endless and circular debates. Categorizing and cataloging helps us to understand and appreciate what something is by separating it from what it isn't. It's not cold-hearted or narrow-minded to suggest that a bird is not a fish. It's actually quite useful if someone is interested in studying birds. The same is true here. Once the boundaries of stories are drawn, you can suddenly see the theoretical and practical details of the artform at a new level of approximation. You can study the details, threads, connections, and elements and by doing so, come to some important conclusions about how these pieces work in unison to tie stories together.

You can also notice something else. You can see that stories, as strategic communication instruments, can be adapted to fit particular situations. Like reaching into a toolbox to find the right tool that's needed, various situations match with particular stories. This book has proposed that there are eight stories that can be supremely effective depending on the needs of a specific business scenario. Assess the situation, then consider which story format best responds to the need. I have tried to describe each of these story formats in detail, steering clear of clichés, noting that with the help of The Base we can select and modify story elements to maximize effectiveness. The stories described in chapter 3—The Maker, The Vision, The Product, The Springboard, The Morale Builder, the Capsule, and The Talk—all have elements in common. Their differences, however, speak to the job at hand. By using these formats and the advice mentioned in the harvesting section, you can blueprint stories without feeling unsure about your footing. You can build stories witg confidence, knowing that you have a overall structure in place that will never fail you. After all, storytelling is your superpower. This book merely highlights information that your DNA already holds.

I wish you the best in your storytelling journey and I hope you give the techniques in this book a chance to work for you. Your business presentations can take on an entirely new dimension if these strategies are implemented. Not only that, but learning more about story structure has ramifications across a whole spectrum of intellectually and emotionally enriching activities. Stories provide deep insight into our own lives by stepping into the shoes of another person's predicament. In the pursuit of a more just, equitable, tolerant, and prosperous world, perhaps nothing is more important than that invitation of the mind.

For more on Tall Tales, India's leading storytelling organization and creator of South Asia's most popular writing workshop, see talltales.in.

***

As a way of encouraging you to take story notes right here, I've included some extra pages for your use.

www.ingramcontent.com/pod-product-compliance
Lightning Source LLC
LaVergne TN
LVHW091219080426
835509LV00009B/1080